Melbourne
& Southeast
Australia

Darroch Donald

D0226479

Credits

Footprint credits
Editorial: Felicity Laughton
Maps: Kevin Feeney

Managing Director: Andy Riddle
Commercial Director: Patrick Dawson
Publisher: Alan Murphy
Publishing Managers: Felicity Laughton,
Jo Williams, Nicola Gibbs
Marketing and Parnerships Director:
Liz Harper
Trade Product Manager: Diane McEntee
Account Managers: Paul Bew, Tania Ross
Advertising: Renu Sibal, Elizabeth Taylor
Trade Product Co-ordinator: Kirsty Holmes

Photography credits
Front cover: Twelve Apostles, Great Ocean
Road, Kimeveruss/iStockphoto
Back cover: Webb Bridge, Docklands,
Melbourne, Shutterstock.com

Printed in Great Britain by CPI Antony Rowe,
Chippenham, Wiltshire

Publishing information
Footprint *Focus Melbourne and
Southeast Australia*
1st edition
© Footprint Handbooks Ltd
August 2012

ISBN: 978 1 908206 76 3
CIP DATA: A catalogue record for this book
is available from the British Library

® Footprint Handbooks and the Footprint
mark are a registered trademark of Footprint
Handbooks Ltd

Published by Footprint
6 Riverside Court,
Lower Bristol Road, Bath BA2 3DZ, UK
T +44 (0)1225 469141
F +44 (0)1225 469461
www.footprinttravelguides.com

nt *Focus Melbourne*
has been taken
Eve ... s *East Coast Australia*
the ... esearched and
Hov ... nald.
fror
anc

The
resp
inco

Contents

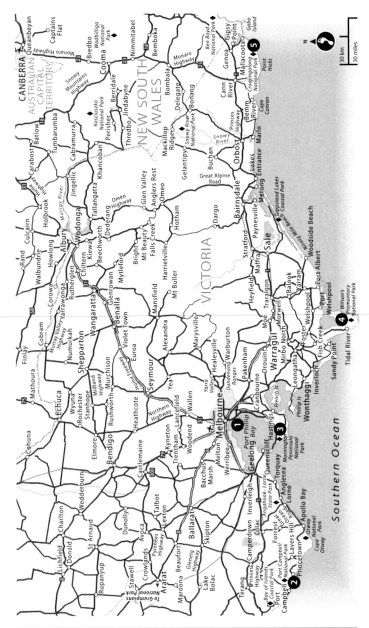

Victoria is Australia's smallest and most populous mainland state. By Australian standards, you could almost say it is crowded. Despite its size, however, it is incredibly diverse: mountains, deserts, rainforest, beaches and plains make up the landscape. The state also has a rich historical heritage, multicultural people and a large sophisticated city.

The state revolves around Melbourne, a city that combines the gracious character of its Victorian past with style, innovation and energy. Not only is Melbourne pretty to look at, with its beautiful parks and gardens and its serpentine Yarra River, but it is the most cosmopolitan of all Australian cities, with a huge cultural mix.

Within just an hour or two of Australia's second largest city, you can swim with dolphins or try local wines in the Yarra Valley. To the west are the popular coastal towns of the Great Ocean Road. Inland is one of the state's best national parks, the magnificent Grampians, where craggy sandstone rockfaces tower above swathes of forest. Towards the coast the foothills run down to the moist green fields of Gippsland and come to an end in the perfect sandy coves of Wilson's Promontory and the series of tranquil lakes, lagoons and inlets further east.

Planning your trip

Best time to visit Melbourne and Southeast Australia

One of the joys of the East Coast is that at any time of year there is always some section where the weather is just right. The converse, of course, is that those particular about their destination need good timing. Due to its southerly position Victoria is the coldest and wettest state, especially in winter. However, that said, inland areas of the state (including Melbourne) can get very hot in summer (hotter than Sydney) with much of the interior currently sharing the protracted drought issues of New South Wales and Queensland. The heightened variance in Victoria's climate is due to the influence of northerly winds from the interior and the ocean-borne influences from the south and west. The former, known as the 'southerly change', is essentially Victorian for 'put the fire on and find the umbrella'. Melbourne is famous for its 'four seasons in one day' with a southerly change from a northerly influence seeing the temperature drop dramatically by over 20°C, often with lively thunderstorms.

In 2009 Victoria's extremes were highlighted when, in February, temperatures reached 46°C in and around Melbourne. This was a pivotal factor that led to Australia's worst natural disaster, 'Black Saturday', when fires raged around the state with the loss of over 173 lives and 2000 properties.

Broadly speaking, the peak season between Sydney and Brisbane is from mid-December to the end of January. Conversely autumn to spring (March to October) is considered the peak season north of Rockhampton (Tropic of Capricorn), when dry, warm weather is the norm. The 'stinger season' between October and May also presents its own dangers (jellyfish). Generally, accommodation and tourist sites in all three states stay open year round, the main exceptions being in the far north in midsummer (December to March).

Watch out for school holidays and peak seasons, when some areas get completely booked out months in advance (particularly between Sydney and Brisbane). School holidays tend to take place from mid-December to late January, a week or two around Easter, a couple of weeks in June and July and another couple during September and October. If planning a long trip, say three months or more, try to make spring or autumn the core of your time. Also note that during big sporting events such as cricket (summer) and rugby tests (winter) as well as the Aussie Rules football finals (again in spring, especially in Victoria), you are strongly advised to book transport tickets and accommodation as far ahead as possible. ▸▸ *See Public holidays, page 20.*

Climate

As a general rule of thumb, the further north you travel, and the further in time from July, the hotter it gets. And hot means very hot: days over 40°C regularly occur in summer in the arid regions and even cities as far south as Melbourne average around 25°C. In the north of the country summer (November to April) is synonymous with 'the wet', a period characterized by high humidity, heat, tremendous monsoonal rainfall and occasional, powerful cyclones. Periods of prolonged showers, particularly late in the wet season, are also common. Australia is the driest inhabited continent and most areas are currently

Don't miss ...

1 **Federation Square**, page 27.
2 **12 apostles, Great Ocean Road**, page 40.
3 **Mornington Peninsula**, page 35.
4 **Wilson's Promontory**, page 60.
5 **Croajingolong National Park**, page 62.

Numbers relate to the map on page 4.

suffering the longest and most protracted drought on record. Drought or no drought, virtually nowhere further than 250 km inland gets more than an average of 600 mm of rain a year. About half the continent, in a band across the south and west, gets less than 300 mm and much of it is desert. Naturally, the East Coast and elevated areas along the Great Divide see much higher rainfall. For comprehensive weather forecasts, see www.bom.gov.au.

Getting to Melbourne and Southeast Australia

Air

There are international flights direct to Melbourne, Sydney, Brisbane and Cairns and it is quite possible to have different points of arrival and departure that complement your intended itinerary. If there is not a direct flight to your primary choice there will usually be a same-day connection from Sydney or Melbourne. It is usually possible to book internal Australian flights when booking your international ticket, at lower prices than on arrival. Some do not even require a stated departure and arrival point. If you have any plans to fly within New South Wales or Queensland check this out prior to booking.

Fares depend on the season, with prices higher during December and January unless booked well in advance. Mid-year sees the cheapest fares. **Qantas**, www.qantas.com.au, is Australia's main international and domestic airline and flies from most international capitals and major cities. That said, with the advent of the global financial crisis, competition is fiercer than ever, and Qantas is struggling in international and domestic markets against other airlines like Emirates, V Australia and Tiger Airways. Most other international major airlines have flights to Australia from their home countries.

Airport information

Melbourne, Sydney, Brisbane and Cairns are the main airports and all have excellent services. All the main airlines fly to these airports with regular connections from international and national destinations. Facilities are good and include banks, ATMs and tourist offices where help is on hand with booking accommodation and organizing tours and transport. All the airports offer regular and efficient connections with the city centres either by coach or rail. See the respective sections for further details or refer to www.melbourneairport.com.au; www.sydneyairport.com.au and www.bne.com.au.

Transport in Melbourne and Southeast Australia

Public transport is generally good and efficient and often easier than driving. Most cities have good metropolitan bus services, though some are curiously unaware of tourist traffic and there is many an important outlying attraction poorly served by public transport, or even missed off the bus routes completely. Some cities are compact enough for this to be a minor irritation, others are so spread out that the visitor must invest in an expensive tourist bus service or taxis. In such places staying at a hostel or B&B with free or low-cost bike hire can save a lot of money. Bear in mind that when it comes to public transport in the major centres, Australia is hardly comparable to Japan or to a lesser extent Europe or North America. In cities like Melbourne, if you ask a local to comment on their public transport system, the reply will be a few choice words and a considerable degree of frustration and anger.

By far the best way of seeing the East Coast is under your own steam, or with a tour operator with an in-depth itinerary. See Tours operators in individual town and city sections for details. The further from the cities you go, the more patchy and irregular public transport becomes. All the states have networks based on a combination of air, bus and train. Some of these services connect up at border towns but check first. If you are short on time and long on funds, flying can save a lot of time, money and effort, both interstate and within New South Wales and Queensland. In some cases it is the only real option. Most other interstate options involve long-distance buses, and on a few routes, trains. Train fares and domestic air travel can be considerably cheaper if booked in advance and on the net. For flights within Australia, try www.webjet.com.au.

Air

Qantas, T131313, www.qantas.com.au, **Tiger Airways**, T03-9335 3033, www.tigerairways.com, Jetstar, T131538, www.jetstar.com.au, and **Virgin Blue**, T136789, www.virginblue.com.au, link most state capitals to each other and to many of the larger towns and main tourist destinations. There are also several regional airways operating smaller planes on specialist routes including **Regional Express (REX)**, T131713, www.regionalexpress.com.au. Domestic fares have dropped dramatically in recent years. In 2009 a one-way ticket between Melbourne and Sydney was available for as little as $40 and for Sydney to Cairns for $175. But bear in mind with budget airlines this does not take into account cargo baggage, for which you will pay significantly more. For up-to-date information on whether a destination is served by scheduled or charter flights, contact your destination's tourist office or each airline direct.

Bear in mind that many provincial airports may not be staffed when you arrive. Check with the local tourist office regarding transport from the airport to the town.

Rail

Train travel up and down the East Coast is a viable mode of transport and can be a delightful way to get from A to B, especially if you are short of time. Given the distances between the main centres, Australia lends itself to rail travel and you may find routes with such evocative names as **Sunlander** and **Spirit of the Outback** irresistible. That said, a car or coach is a better option if you wish to explore or get off the beaten track. The East Coast offers endless beaches and numerous national parks that are well away from any railway stations. Also bear in mind that track gauges differ in NSW and Queensland, so the crossing between the two takes in an intriguing transition by road. Also, note that overnight travel by rail is possible, though often expensive, if you wish to have the comfort of your own compartment and to do it in style. Well worth considering is a jaunt into the outback from Brisbane to Longreach on board the Spirit of the Outback.

In New South Wales, Countrylink, T132232 (within Australia), www.countrylink. nsw.gov.au, offers rail and rail/coach services state-wide and to Brisbane. There are several Countrylink travel centres at principal stations in Sydney including the Sydney Central Railway Station, T02-99379 3800. A useful website for travel throughout New South Wales is www.webwombat.com.au/transport/nsw.htm.

In Queensland, Queensland Rail, T131617, www.qr.com.au, offers a range of rail services up and down the coast and into the outback. Brisbane (Roma Street) Transit Centre in Brisbane, T07-3236 2528, hosts offices for most major coach and rail service providers and is a fine source of general travel information. Outback Queensland is also well served by all of the above but stopovers and less frequent travel schedules are obviously the norm.

In Victoria state, V-Line, T136196, www.vline.com.au, is the principal service provider.

Road

Bus State and interstate bus services offer the most cost-effective way of constructing an itinerary for a single traveller. A large selection of bus services can be found at www.buslines.com.au. Always check the journey duration and time of arrival, as some routes can take days, with just a couple of short meal stops. Many coaches are equipped with videos but you may also want something to read. It's also a good idea to take warm clothing, socks, a pillow, toothbrush and earplugs. There's a good chance you'll arrive in the late evening or the early hours of the morning. If so, book accommodation ahead and, if possible, transfer transportation.

The main operator throughout New South Wales and Queensland is Greyhound Pioneer, T1300 473946, www.greyhound.com.au (referred to simply as Greyhound throughout this guide), while in Victoria the principal service provider is V-Line, T136196, www.vline.com.au. Their networks follow all the main interstate highways up and down the coast with offshoots including the Blue Mountains, New England (Hunter Valley), Armidale, Charters Towers, the Atherton Tablelands and so on. As well as scheduled routes, they offer a range of passes. There are also many other smaller regional companies. Most are listed under the relevant destinations. Countrylink, T132232, www.countrylink.info, also offers coach services to some centres in conjunction with rail schedules between New South Wales and Queensland.

Greyhound offer a wide variety of passes with several jump-on, jump-off options. The Day Passes system has three options: the Standard Day Pass allows you to travel anywhere on the Greyhound network for the number of consecutive days you choose with a pre-set kilometre limit. You can buy a pass for three days (1000 km limit, $154), five days (1500 km limit, $223), seven days (2000 km limit, $286), 10 days (3000 km limit, $398), 20 days (6000 km limit, $755), 30 days (10,000 km, $1030). The Flexi Day Pass gives you total flexibility without a kilometre restriction. Customers purchase the number of days' travel required (10, 15 or 21) and have up to 60 days to use the travelling days purchased, while The Fixed Day Pass gives you freedom to travel for a consecutive number of days (10, 15 and 21) without a kilometre restriction.

The Explorer Pass commits you to a set one-way or circular route and is valid for between 30 and 365 days. There are a couple of dozen options including Best of the East, which takes in Cairns to Melbourne and the Red Centre at around $1451, and an All Australian at $2988.

Other passes include the **Mini Traveller**, which provides travel between two popular destinations; in between you can hop on and hop off as much as you like in the one direction, over 45 days. From Cairns to Sydney will cost around $408.

Backpacker buses There are now several operators who make the assumption that the most important part of your trip is the journey. These companies combine the roles of travel operator and tour guide, taking from two to five times longer than scheduled services (a good indicator of just how much they get off the highway). They are worth considering, especially if you are travelling alone. In terms of style, price ($95-175 per day) and what is included, they vary greatly and it is important to clarify this prior to booking. Some offer transport and commentary only, others include accommodation and some meals, a few specialize in 4WD and bush camping. A few, including **Oz Experience** (see below) offer jump-on, jump-off packages and are priced more on distance. The popular option of flying Sydney to Cairns independently and then returning by bus (or vice versa) is also worth considering and would cost about $675. The main backpacker bus company in NSW and Queensland is **Oz Experience**, T1300 300028, www.ozexperience.com.

Car If you live in a small and populous country, travelling by car in Australia will be an enlightening experience, as well as an enervating one. Distances are huge and travelling times between the major cities, towns and sights can seem endless, so put on some tunes and make driving part of the whole holiday experience.

You should consider buying a car if you are travelling for more than three months. Consider a campervan if hiring or buying. Traffic congestion is rarely an issue on the East Coast route – only Sydney has anything like the traffic of many other countries, so driving itineraries can be based on covering a planned distance each day, up to, say, 100 km for each solid hour's driving. The key factor in planning is distance. It is pretty stress-free and as the distances can be huge, drivers can get bored and sleepy. There are a lot of single-vehicle accidents in Australia, many the result of driver fatigue.

The other major factor when planning is the type of roads you may need to use. Almost all the main interstate highways between Sydney and Cairns are 'sealed', though there are a few exceptions. Many country roads are unsealed, usually meaning a stony or sand surface. When recently graded (levelled and compacted) they can be almost as pleasant to drive on as sealed roads, but even then there are reduced levels of handling. After grading, unsealed roads deteriorate over time. Potholes form, they can become impassable when wet and corrugations usually develop, especially on national park roads, with heavy usage. These are regular ripples in the road surface, at right angles to the road direction, that can go on for tens of kilometres. Small ones simply cause an irritating judder, large ones can reduce tolerable driving speeds to 10-20 kph. Generally, the bigger the wheel size and the longer the wheel base, the more comfortable the journey over corrugations will be. Many unsealed roads can be negotiated with a two-wheel drive (2WD) low-clearance vehicle but the ride will be a lot more comfortable, and safer, in a 4WD high-clearance one. Most 2WD hire cars are uninsured if driven on unsealed roads. Some unsealed roads (especially in the outback) are designated as 4WD-only or tracks, though individual definitions can differ according to the map or authority you consult. If in doubt, stick to the roads you are certain are safe for your vehicle and you are sufficiently prepared for. With careful preparation, however, and the right vehicles (convoys are recommended), traversing the major outback tracks is an awesome experience.

If you stray far from the coast, and certainly anywhere outback, prepare carefully. Carry essential spares and tools such as fan belts, hoses, gaffer tape, a tyre repair kit, extra car jack, extra spare wheel and tyre, spade, decent tool kit, oil and coolant and a fuel can. Membership of the NRMA (NSW) or the RACQ (QLD) is recommended (see below), as is informing someone of your intended itinerary. Above all carry plenty of spare water, at least 10 litres per person, 20 if possible. As far as the best make of vehicle for the outback, in Australia it is the iconic Toyota Landcruiser every time. Break down in a cruiser and the chances are spare parts can be sourced quite easily, without waiting days for foreign hard-to-come-by items. Break down in a Mitsubishi Delica and you may as well look for a job and get married to a local.

Rules and regulations To drive in Australia you must have a current driving licence. Foreign nationals also need an international driving licence, available from your national motoring organization. In Australia you drive on the left. Speed limits vary between states, with maximum urban limits of 50-60 kph and maximum country limits of 100-120 kph. Speeding penalties include a fine and police allow little leeway. Seatbelts are compulsory for drivers and passengers. Driving under the influence of alcohol is illegal over certain (very small) limits and penalties are severe.

Petrol costs Fuel costs are approximately half that in Britain and twice that in the US, but due to the recent increase in the price of crude are following the global trend and rising rapidly. In mid-2010 they were fluctuating between $1.20 and $1.30 a litre in city centres and marginally more in the outback. Diesel was traditionally more expensive than unleaded at about $1.35, but it's less prone to price fluctuations and in recent times can actually beat unleaded at a more consistent $1.20. When budgeting, allow at least $15 for every estimated 100 km. A trip around the eastern circuit can easily involve driving 20,000 km. Picking an economical vehicle and conserving fuel can save hundreds of dollars.

Motoring organizations Every state has a breakdown service that is affiliated to the **Australian Automobile Association (AAA)**, www.aaa.asn.au, with which your home country organization may have a reciprocal link. You need to join one of the state associations: in New South Wales **NRMA**, T132132, www.nrma.com.au, in Victoria **RACV**, T131329, www.racv.com.au, and in Queensland **RACQ**, T131905, www.racq.com.au. Note also that you may be covered for only about 100 km (depending on the scheme) of towing distance and that without cover towing services are very expensive. Given the sheer distances you are likely to cover by car, joining an automobile organization is highly recommended but read the fine print with regard to levels of membership in relation to coverage outside metropolitan areas and in the outback.

Vehicle hire Car rental costs vary considerably according to where you hire from (it's cheaper in the big cities, though small local companies can have good deals), what you hire and the mileage/insurance terms. You may be better off making arrangements in your own country for a fly/drive deal. Watch out for kilometre caps: some can be as low as 100 km per day. The minimum you can expect to pay in Australia is around $250 a week for a small car. Drivers need to be over 21. At peak times it can be impossible to get a car at short notice and some companies may dispose of a booked car within as little as half an hour of you not showing up for an agreed pick-up time. If you've booked a car but are going to be late, ensure that you let them know before the pick-up time.

Cycling Long-term bicycle hire is rarely available and touring cyclists should plan to bring their own bike or buy in Australia. Bicycle hire is available in most towns and cities and companies are listed in the relevant sections of this book. If you do plan on touring the coast by bicycle, the website www.cycling.org.au is recommended.

Hitchhiking Hitchhiking, while not strictly illegal in New South Wales and Queensland, is not advised by anyone. The tragic events near Barrow Creek in 2001 demonstrate that there will always be twisted souls who will assault or abduct people for their own evil ends. This is not to say that hitching is more dangerous in Australia than elsewhere else.

Maps

Several publishers produce hard-copy countrywide and state maps. Regional maps are also available and the most useful for general travel. The best and cheapest of these are generally published by each state's motoring organization, see page 11. Road and street maps for all the major Australian regions, cities and towns can be found at www.ltl.com.au/sydneymapshop.htm.

AUSLIG, the national mapping agency, publishes 54 x 54 km topographical maps, at 1:100,000 scale, of every area in Australia, recommended for any long-distance trekking or riding. Most areas are now in print, but if not black and white copies can be obtained. For a map index, place name search, details of distributors or mail order, contact T1800 800173, www.auslig.gov.au. AUSLIG also publishes a 1:250,000 series, covering the whole country, useful for those heading outback on 4WD trips. If you're thinking of tackling one of the major outback tracks, such as the Great Central Road, Tanami, Birdsville or Strzelecki, then get hold of the appropriate map published by **Westprint**, T03-5391 1466, www.westprint.com.au, which is the acknowledged expert in this field.

In the cities it is worth getting hold of a mini version of the street map tomes. In Sydney it is **Sydway**, Melbourne **Melway** and Brisbane, yes you got it, **Brisway**. Sadly, being so small, there is no 'TittyBongWay', or indeed 'WaggaWaggaWay'. Shame.

Recommended outlets are given throughout the book, listed in the Shopping sections for the larger towns and cities. Specialist map shops to contact or visit before your trip include the following outlets (who also offer online shopping): **Stanfords**, 12-14 Longacre, London, WC2E 9LP, T020-7836 1321, www.stanfords. co.uk; and **Rand McNally**, 150E 52nd Street, Midtown East, New York, T212-758 7488, www.randmcnally.com.

And of course, to really whet your appetite, it's worth a muse online with **Google Earth**, especially for Sydney, Melbourne and places like the Blue Mountains, Fraser Island and the Great Barrier Reef.

Where to stay in Melbourne and Southeast Australia

East Coast Australia presents a diverse and attractive range of accommodation options, from cheap national park campsites to luxurious retreats. The real beauty here, given the weather and the environment, is that travelling on a budget does not detract from the enjoyment of the trip. On the contrary, this is a place where a night under canvas in any of the national parks is an absolute delight.

Booking accommodation in advance is highly recommended, especially in peak seasons. Booking online will usually secure the best rates. Check if your accommodation has airC conditioning (a/c) when booking. Rooms without air conditioning are almost impossible to sleep in during hot weather. Note that single rooms are relatively scarce. Twin or double rooms let to a single occupant are rarely half the price and you may even be charged the full cost for two people.

Hotels, lodges, motels and resorts
At the top end of the scale, especially in the state capital, there are some impressive international-standard hotels, lodges and resorts, with luxurious surroundings and facilities, attentive service and often outstanding locations.

Rooms in hotels and lodges will typically start in our **$$$$** range. In the main cities are a few less expensive hotels in the **$$$** range. Most 'hotels' outside of the major towns are pubs with upstairs or external accommodation. If upstairs, a room is likely to have access to shared bathroom facilities, while external rooms are usually standard en suite motel units. The quality of pub-hotel accommodation varies considerably but is usually a budget option (**$$**). Linen is almost always supplied.

Motels in Australia are usually depressingly anonymous but dependably clean and safe and offer the cheapest en suite rooms. Most have dining facilities and free, secure parking. Some fall into our **$$** range, most will be a **$$$-$$**. Linen is always supplied.

B&Bs and self-catering
Bed and breakfast (B&B) is in some ways quite different from the British model. Not expensive, but rarely a budget option, most fall into our **$$$-$$** ranges. They offer very comfortable accommodation in usually upmarket, sometimes historic houses. Rooms are usually en suite or have access to a private bathroom. Most hosts are friendly and informative. Some B&Bs are actually semi or fully self-contained cottages or cabins with breakfast provisions supplied. Larger ones may have full kitchens. As well as private houses, caravan parks and hostels and some resorts and motels provide self-contained, self-catering options with apartment-style units. Linen may not be supplied in self-catering accommodation.

A couple of good websites are www.bedandbreakfast.com.au, www.bbbook.com.au.

National parks, farms and stations

Some national parks and rural cattle and sheep stations have old settlers' or workers' homes that have been converted into tourist accommodation, which is usually self-contained. They are often magical places to stay and include many old lighthouse keepers' cottages and shearers' quarters. Stations may also invite guests to watch, or even get involved in, the day's activities. Transport to them can be difficult if you don't have your own vehicle. Linen is often not supplied in this sort of accommodation.

Hostels

For those travelling on a tight budget there is a large network of hostels offering cheap accommodation (**$$-$**). These are also popular centres for backpackers and provide great opportunities for meeting fellow travellers. All hostels have kitchen and common room facilities, almost all now have internet and some have considerably more. A few, particularly in cities, will offer freebies including breakfast and pick-ups. Many are now open 24 hours, even if the front desk is closed at night. Standards vary considerably and it's well worth asking the opinions of other travellers. Most are effectively independent – even most YHAs are simply affiliates – but the best tend to be those that are owner-managed. Of several hostel associations, **YHA**, www.yha.org.au, and NOMADS, T02-9299 7710, www.nomadsworld.com, no membership fee, seem to keep the closest eye on their hostels, ensuring a consistency of quality. The **YMCA**, T03-9699 7655, www.ymca.org.au, and YWCA, T02-6230 5150, www.ywca.org.au, are usually a clean and quiet choice in the major cities. International visitors can obtain a **Hostelling International Card** (HIC) from any YHA hostel or travel centre: it's valid for one year and costs $32. For this you get a handbook of YHA hostels nationwide and around $3 off every night's accommodation. Some transport and tourist establishments also offer discounts to HIC holders. For more information, see www.hihostels.com.

Caravan and tourist parks

Almost every town will have at least one caravan park, with unpowered and powered sites varying from $25-40 (for two) for campers, caravans and campervans, an ablutions block and usually a camp kitchen or barbecues. Some will have permanently sited caravans (onsite vans) and cabins. Onsite vans are usually the cheapest option (**$**) for families or small groups wanting to self-cater. Cabins are usually more expensive (**$$**). Some will have televisions, en suite bathrooms, separate bedrooms with linen and well-equipped kitchens. Power is rated at the domestic level (240/250v AC), which is very convenient for budget travellers. Some useful organizations are: **Big 4**, T0300-738044 / T03-9811 9300, www.big4.com.au; **Family Parks of Australia**, T02-6021 0977, www.familyparks.com.au; and **Top Tourist Parks**, T08-8363 1901, www.toptourist.contact.com.au. Joining a park association will get you a discount in all parks that are association members.

If you intend to use motor parks, get hold of the latest editions of the tourist park guides published by the NMRA, RACV and RACQ. They are an essential resource.

Price codes

Where to stay

$$$$ over AU$200   **$$$** AU$110-200

$$ AU$50-109   **$**   under AU$50

Prices include taxes and service charge, but not meals. They are based on a double room, except in the **$** range, where prices are almost always per person.

Restaurants

$$$ over AU$35   **$$** AU$25-35   **$** under AU$25

Prices refer to the cost of a two-course meal, not including drinks.

Camping

Bush camping is the best way to experience the natural environment. Some national parks allow camping, mostly in designated areas only, with a few allowing limited bush camping. Facilities are usually minimal, with basic toilets, fireplaces and perhaps tank water; a few have barbecues and shower blocks. Payment is often by self-registration (around $6-15 per person) and barbecues often require $0.20, $0.50 or $1 coins, so have small notes and change ready. In many parks you will need a gas stove. If there are fireplaces you must bring your own wood as collecting wood within parks is prohibited. No fires may be lit, even stoves, during a total fire ban. Even if water is supposedly available it is not guaranteed so take a supply, as well as your own toilet paper. Camping in the national parks is strictly regulated. For details of the various rules, contact Parks Victoria, www.parkweb.vic.gov.au.

Campervans

A popular choice for many visitors is to hire or buy a vehicle that can be slept in, combining the costs of accommodation and transport (although you will still need to book into caravan parks for power and ablutions). Ranging from the popular VW Kombi to enormous vans with integral bathrooms, they can be hired from as little as $60 per day to a de luxe 4WD model for as much as $800. A van for two people at around $130 per day compares well with hiring a car and staying in hostels and allows greater freedom. High-clearance, 4WD campervans are also available and increase travel possibilities yet further. Kombis can usually be bought from about $2500. An even cheaper, though less comfortable, alternative is to buy a van or station wagon (estate car) from around $2000 that is big enough to lay out a sleeping mat and bag in.

Sales outlets Apollo, T+800 3260 5466, www.apollocarrentals.com.au; **Backpacker**, T03-8379 8893, www.backpackercampervans.com; **Britz**, T03-8379 8890, www.britz.com.au; Getabout, T02-9380 5536, www.getaboutoz.com; **Maui**, T03-8379 8891 (T800 2008 0801), www.maui.com.au; **Wicked**, T07-3634 9000, www.wickedcampers.com.au. The latter are proving immensely popular with the backpacker set and you will see their vivid, arty vans everywhere. However, they may not suit everybody (you'll see what we mean).

Food and drink in Melbourne and Southeast Australia

The quintessential image of Australian cooking may be of throwing some meat on the barbie but Australia actually has a dynamic and vibrant cuisine all its own. Freed from the bland English 'meat and two veg' straitjacket in the 1980s by the skills and cuisines of Chinese, Thai, Vietnamese, Italian, Greek, Lebanese and other immigrants, Australia has developed a fusion cuisine that takes elements from their cultures and mixes them into something new and original.

Asian ingredients are easily found in major cities because of the country's large Asian population. Australia makes its own dairy products so cheese or cream may come from Tasmania's King Island, Western Australia's Margaret River or the Atherton Tablelands in Far North Queensland. There is plenty of seafood, including some unfamiliar creatures such as the delicious Moreton bugs (crabs), yabbies and crayfish. Mussels, oysters and abalone are all also harvested locally. Fish is a treat too: snapper, dhufish, coral trout and red emperor or the dense, flavoursome flesh of freshwater fish such as barramundi and Murray cod. Freshness is a major feature of modern Australian cuisine, using local produce and cooking it simply to preserve the intrinsic flavour. Native animals are used, such as kangaroo, emu and crocodile, and native plants that Aboriginal people have been eating for thousands of years such as quandong, wattle seed or lemon myrtle leaf. A word of warning, however: this gourmet experience is mostly restricted to cities and large towns. There are pockets of foodie heaven in the country but these are usually associated with wine regions and are the exception rather than the rule.

Eating out

Eating habits in Australia are essentially the same as in most Western countries and are of course affected by the climate. The barbecue on the beach or in the back garden is an Aussie classic but you will find that most eating out during daylight hours takes place outdoors. Weekend brunch is hugely popular, especially in the cities, and often takes up the whole morning. Melbourne is the undisputed gourmet capital, where you will find the very best of modern Australian cuisine as well as everything from Mexican to Mongolian, Jamaican to Japanese. Restaurants are common even in the smallest towns, but the smaller the town the lower the quality, though not usually the price. Chinese and Thai restaurants are very common, with most other cuisines appearing only in the larger towns and cities. Corporate hotels and motels almost all have attached restaurants, as do traditional pubs, which also serve counter meals. Some may have a more imaginative menu or better quality fare than the local restaurants. Most restaurants are licensed, others BYO only, in which case you provide wine or beer and the restaurant provides glasses. Despite the corkage fee this still makes for a better deal than paying the huge mark-up on alcohol. Sadly, Australians have taken to fast food as enthusiastically as anywhere else in the world. Alongside these are food courts, found in the shopping malls of cities and larger towns. Also in the budget bracket are the delis and milk bars, serving hot takeaways together with sandwiches, cakes and snacks.

Drinks

Australian **wine** will need no introduction to most readers. Many of the best-known labels, including **Penfolds** and **Jacob's Creek**, are produced in South Australia but there are dozens of recognized wine regions right across the southern third of Australia, where the climate is favourable for grape growing and the soil sufficient to produce high-standard grapes. The industry has a creditable history in such a young country, with several wineries boasting a tradition of a century or more, but it is only in the last 25 years that Australia has become one of the major players on the international scene, due in part to its variety and quality. There are no restrictions, as there are in parts of Europe, on what grape varieties are grown where, when they are harvested and how they are blended.

Visiting a winery is an essential part of any visit to the country, and a day or two's tasting expedition is a scenic and cultural as well as an epicurean delight. Cellar doors range from modern marble and glass temples to venerable, century-old former barns of stone and wood, often boasting some of the best restaurants in the country. In New South Wales the Hunter Valley provides one of the best vineyard experiences in the world with more than a 100 wineries, world-class B&Bs and tours ranging from cycling to horse-drawn carriage.

Australians themselves drink more and more wine and less beer. The average rate of consumption is now 20 litres per person per year, compared to eight litres in 1970. Beer has dropped from an annual 135 litres per person in 1980 to 95 litres now. The price of wine, however, is unexpectedly high given the relatively low cost of food and beer. Visitors from Britain will find Australian wines hardly any cheaper at the cellar door than back home in the supermarket.

The vast majority of **beer** drunk by Australians is lager, despite often being called 'ale' or 'bitter'. The big brands such as **VB** (Victoria), **Tooheys** (NSW) and **Castlemaine XXXX** (QLD) are fairly homogenous but refreshing on a hot day. If your palate is just a touch more refined, hunt out some of the imported beers on tap that are predominantly found in the pseudo-Irish pubs in almost all the main coastal towns. Beer tends to be around 4-5% alcohol, with the popular and surprisingly pleasant-tasting 'mid' varieties about 3.5%, and 'light' beers about 2-2.5%. Drink driving laws are strict and the best bet is to not drink alcohol at all if you are driving. As well as being available on draught in pubs, beer can also be bought from bottleshops (bottle-o's) in cases (slabs) of 24-36 cans (tinnies or tubes) or bottles (stubbies) of 375 ml each. This is by far the cheapest way of buying beer (often under $4 per can or bottle).

Essentials A-Z

Accident and emergency
Dial 000 for the emergency services. The 3 main professional emergency services are supported by several others, including the **State Emergency Service (SES)**, **Country Fire Service (CFS)**, **Surf Life Saving Australia (SLSA)**, **Sea-search and Rescue** and **St John's Ambulance**. The SES is prominent in coordinating search and rescue operations. The CFS provides invaluable support in fighting and controlling bush fires. These services, though professionally trained, are mostly provided by volunteers.

Electricity
The current in Australia is 240/250v AC. Plugs have 2- or 3-blade pins and adaptors are widely available.

Embassies and high commissions
For a list of Australian embassies and high commissions worldwide, see www.embassy.gov.au.

Health
Before you go
Ideally, you should see your GP or travel clinic at least 6 weeks before your departure for general advice on travel risks, malaria and vaccinations. No vaccinations are required or recommended for travel to Australia unless travelling from a yellow fever-infected country in Africa or South America. Check with your local Australian Embassy for further advice. A tetanus booster is advisable, however, if you have one due. Make sure you have travel insurance, get a dental check (especially if you are going to be away for more than a month), know your own blood group and, if you suffer a long-term condition such as diabetes or epilepsy, make sure someone knows or that you have a Medic Alert bracelet/necklace with this information on it.

A-Z of health risks
There are 3 main threats to health in Australia: the powerful sun, dengue fever and poisonous snakes and spiders.

For **sun protection**, a decent wide-brimmed hat and factor 30 suncream (cheap in Australian supermarkets) are essential. Follow the Australians with their Slip, Slap, Slop campaign: slip on a shirt, slap on a hat and slop on the sunscreen.

Dengue can be contracted throughout Australia. In travellers this can cause a severe flu-like illness, which includes symptoms of fever, lethargy, enlarged lymph glands and muscle pains. It starts suddenly, lasts for 2-3 days, seems to get better for 2-3 days and then kicks in again for another 2-3 days. It is usually all over in an unpleasant week. The mosquitoes that carry the dengue virus bite during the day, unlike the malaria mosquitoes, which sadly means that repellent application and covered limbs are a 24-hr issue. Check your accommodation for flower pots and shallow pools of water since these are where the dengue-carrying mosquitoes breed.

In the case of **snakes and spiders**, check loo seats, boots and the area around you if you're visiting the bush. A bite itself does not mean that anything has been injected into you. However, a commonsense approach is to clean the area of the bite (never have it sutured early on) and get someone to take you to a medical facility fast. The most common poisonous spider is the tiny, shy redback, which has a shiny black body with distinct red markings. It regularly hides under rocks or in garden sheds and garages. Outside toilets are also a favourite. Far more dangerous, though restricted to the Sydney area only, is the Sydney funnel-web, a larger and more aggressive customer, often found in outdoor loos. There are dozens of venomous snake species in Australia. Few are actively aggressive and even those only during certain key times of year, such as mating seasons, but all are easily provoked and for many an untreated bite can be fatal.

Australia has reciprocal arrangements with a few countries allowing citizens of those countries to receive free emergency treatment under the **Medicare** scheme. Citizens of New Zealand and the Republic of Ireland are entitled to free care as public patients in public hospitals and to subsidized medicines under the Pharmaceutical Benefits Scheme. Visitors from Finland, Italy, Malta, the Netherlands, Sweden and the UK also enjoy subsidized out-of-hospital treatment (ie visiting a doctor). If you qualify, contact your own national health scheme to check what documents you will require in Australia to claim **Medicare**. All visitors are, however, strongly advised to take out medical insurance for the duration of their visit.

Money
Currency ➜ *US$1=AU$0.98; £1=AU$1.52; €1=AU$1.19 (Jul 2012).*

All dollars quoted in this guide are Australian unless specified otherwise. The Australian dollar ($) is divided into 100 cents (c). Coins come in denominations of 5c, 10c, 20c, 50c, $1 and $2. Banknotes come in denominations of $5, $10, $20, $50 and $100. The Australian dollar is currently at a record high – almost a dollar for a dollar US and, sadly for Britons, at a 25-year high against the pound.

Banks, ATMs, credit and cash cards
The four major banks, the **ANZ**, **Challenge/ Westpac**, **Commonwealth** and **NAB (National Australia Bank)** are usually the best places to change money and traveller's cheques, though bureaux de change tend to have slightly longer opening hours and often

open at weekends. You can withdraw cash from ATMs with a cash card or credit card issued by most international banks and they can also be used at banks, post offices and bureaux de change. Most hotels, shops, tourist operators and restaurants in Australia accept the major credit cards, though some places may charge for using them. When booking always check if an operator accepts them. EFTPOS (the equivalent of Switch in the UK) is a way of paying for goods and services with a cash card. Unfortunately EFTPOS only works with cards linked directly to an Australian bank account. Bank opening hours are Mon-Fri, from around 0930 to 1630.

Traveller's cheques
The safest way to carry money is in traveller's cheques, though they are fast becoming superseded by the prevalence of credit cards and ATMs. **American Express**, **Thomas Cook** and **Visa** are the cheques most commonly accepted. Remember to keep a record of the cheque numbers and the cheques you've cashed separate from the cheques themselves. Traveller's cheques are accepted for exchange in banks, large hotels, post offices and large gift shops. Some insist that at least a portion of the amount be in exchange for goods or services. Commission when cashing traveller's cheques is usually 1% or a flat rate. Avoid changing money or cheques in hotels as rates are often poor.

Money transfers
If you need money urgently, the quickest way to have it sent is to have it wired to the nearest bank via **Western Union**, T1800 337377, www.travelex.com.au. Charges apply but on a sliding scale. Money can also be wired by **Amex** or **Thomas Cook**, though this may take a day or two, or transferred direct from bank to bank, but this again can take several days. Within Australia use money orders to send money. See www.auspost.com.au.

Cost of travelling

By European, North American and Japanese standards Australia is an inexpensive place to visit. Accommodation, particularly outside the main centres, is good value, though prices can rise uncomfortably in peak seasons. Transport varies considerably in price and can be a major factor in your travelling budget. Eating out can be indecently cheap. There are some restaurants in Sydney comparable with the world's best where $175 is enough to cover dinner for 2 people. The bill at many excellent establishments can be half that. Australian beer is about $4-8 and imported about $6-8 in most pubs and bars, as is a neat spirit or glass of wine. Wine will generally be around 1½ times to double the price in restaurants than it would be from a bottleshop. The minimum budget required, if staying in hostels or campsites, cooking for yourself, not drinking much and travelling relatively slowly, is about $80 per person per day, but this isn't going to be a lot of fun. Going on the odd tour, travelling faster and eating out occasionally will raise this to a more realistic $100-130. Those staying in modest B&Bs, hotels and motels as couples, eating out most nights and taking a few tours will need to reckon on about $220 per person per day. Costs in the major cities will be 20-50% higher. Non-hostelling single travellers should budget on spending around 60-70% of what a couple would spend.

Opening hours

Generally Mon-Fri 0830-1700. Many convenience stores and supermarkets are open daily. Late night shopping is generally either Thu or Fri. For banks, see above.

Post

Most post offices are open Mon-Fri 0900-1700, and Sat 0900-1230. Airmail for postcards and greetings cards is $1.40 anywhere in the world, small letters (under 50 g) are $1.45 to southeast Asia and the Pacific, $2.10 beyond. Parcels can be sent either by sea, economy air or air. Most of the principal or main offices in regional centres or cities offer poste restante for those peripatetic souls with no fixed address, open Mon-Fri 0900-1700. For more information contact **Australia Post** on T131318, www.auspost.com.au.

Public holidays

New Year's Day; **Australia Day** (26 Jan); **Good Friday**; **Easter Monday**; **Anzac Day** (25 Apr); **Queen's Birthday** (Jun); **Labour Day** May in QLD, Oct in NSW; **Christmas Day**; **Boxing (Proclamation) Day**.

Safety

Australia certainly has its dangers, but with a little common sense and basic precautions they are relatively easy to minimize. The most basic but important are the effects of the **sun**, see Health, page 18. In **urban areas**, as in almost any city in the world, there is always the possibility of muggings, alcohol-induced harassment or worse. The usual simple precautions apply, like keeping a careful eye and hand on belongings, not venturing out alone at night and avoiding dark, lonely areas. For information on road safety see page 10, or contact one of the AAA associations, see page 11.

Smoking

This is not permitted in restaurants, cafés or pubs where eating is a primary activity, or on any public transport.

Taxes

Most goods are subject to a **Goods and Services Tax** (GST) of 10%. Some shops can deduct the GST if you have a valid departure ticket. GST on goods over $300 purchased (per store) within 30 days before you leave are refundable on presentation of receipts and purchases at the GST refund booth at Sydney International Airport (boarding pass

State phone codes and time difference

There are no area phone codes. Use a state code if calling outside the state you are in. These are: 02 for ACT/NSW (08 for Broken Hill), 03 for VIC and 07 for QLD. Note that Victoria and NSW operate daylight saving, which means that clocks go forward one hour from October and April.

and passport are also required). For more information, T1300 363263.

Telephone

Most public payphones are operated by nationally owned **Telstra**, www.telstra.com.au. Some take phonecards, available from newsagents and post offices, and credit cards. A payphone call within Australia requires $0.40 or $0.50. If you are calling locally (within approximately 50 km) this lasts indefinitely but only a few seconds, outside the local area. Well worth considering if you are in Australia for any length of time is a pre-paid mobile phone. Telstra and **Vodafone** give the best coverage and their phones are widely available from as little as $150, including some call time. There are also some smaller companies like **'3'** and **Optus** offering attractive deals. By far the cheapest way of calling overseas is to use an international pre-paid phone card (though they cannot be used from a mobile phone, or some of the blue and orange public phones). Available from city post offices and newsagents, every call made with them may initially cost about $1 (a local call plus connection) but subsequent per-minute costs are a fraction of Telstra or mobile phone charges.

There are no area phone codes. Use a state code if calling outside the state you are in. These are: 02 for ACT/ NSW (08 for Broken Hill), 03 for VIC and 07 for QLD. To call Eastern Australia from overseas, dial the international prefix followed by 61, then the state phone code minus the first 0, then the 8-digit number. To call overseas from Australia dial 0011 followed by the country code. Country codes include: Republic of Ireland 353; New Zealand 64; South Africa 27; the USA and Canada 1; the UK 44. Directory enquiries: 1223. International directory enquiries: 1225.

Telephones numbers starting with 1300 or 1800 are toll free within Australia. Where 2 telephone numbers are listed in this guide, this toll-free number appears in brackets.

Time

Australia covers 3 time zones: Queensland and New South Wales are in Eastern Standard GMT+10 hrs. NSW and Victoria operate daylight saving, which means that clocks go forward 1 hr from Oct and Mar.

Tipping

Tipping is not the norm in Australia, but a discretionary 5-10% tip for particularly good service will be appreciated.

Tourist information

Tourist offices, or Visitor Information Centres (VICs), can be found in all but the smallest Australian towns. Generally speaking you are advised to stick with accredited VICs for the best, non-biased advice. Their locations, phone numbers, website or email addresses and opening hours are listed in the relevant sections of this guide. In larger towns they have met certain criteria to be officially accredited. This usually means that they have some paid staff and should be open daily 0900-1700. Smaller offices may close at weekends. All offices will provide information on accommodation, local sights and tours. Many will also have information on eating out, local history and the environment, and will sell souvenirs, guides and maps. Most provide a free town map. Some in high-density tourist destinations like Airlie Beach and Cairns in Queensland also double as privately run booking agencies, but may simply promote those that pay them a booking commission.

The **Australian Tourism Commission** website, www.australia.com, is a good place to start, but almost all regions have excellent, informative websites and these are listed in the relevant areas in the text. Both the national and regional tourist boards and VICs are generally good at replying to specific enquiries, especially by email, and are usually willing to send heaps of useful information by snail mail.

Visas and immigration

Visas are subject to change, so check with your local Australian Embassy or High Commission. For a list of these, see www.embassy.gov.au. All travellers to Australia, except New Zealand citizens, must have a valid visa to enter Australia. These must be arranged prior to travel (allow 2 months) and cannot be organized at Australian airports. Tourist visas are free and are available from your local Australian Embassy or High Commission, or in some countries, in electronic format (an Electronic Travel Authority or ETA) from their websites and from selected travel agents and airlines. Passport holders eligible to apply for an ETA include those from Austria, Belgium, Canada, Denmark, France, Germany, the Irish Republic, Italy, Japan, Netherlands, Norway, Spain, Sweden, Switzerland, the UK and the USA. Tourist visas allow visits of up to 3 months within the year after the visa is issued. Multiple-entry 6-month tourist visas are also available to visitors from certain countries. Application forms can be downloaded from the embassy website or from www.immi.gov.au. Tourist visas do not allow the holder to work in Australia. See also www.immi.gov.au/visitors.

Weights and measures
The metric system is universally used.

Contents

Footprint features

Melbourne & Southeast Australia

Melbourne and around

Melbourne has always been impressive, right from its earliest days when it was the largest, wealthiest and most refined city in the country. This former wealth, reflected in the ornate 19th-century architecture and spacious public gardens, has also bred an innate confidence and serious sophistication that gets right up the noses of Sydneysiders. By the same token, Melbournians see their New South Wales cousins as insufferably brash and hedonistic.

The Victorian capital is the most European of Australia's cities. Its theatres, bookshops and galleries all vibrate with the chatter of cosmopolitan urbanites, and its famously damp, grey weather lends the city an air of introspection lacking in other state capitals. Melbourne is also known as the events capital of Australia, with such high-profile annual extravaganzas as the Melbourne Cup (Spring Carnival) and Grand Prix, together with recent major showcases like the Commonwealth Games in 2006, all raising the international profile of the city – and sending Sydney quietly green with envy.

Arriving in Melbourne → For listings, see pages 42-58.

Getting there

Melbourne's **Tullamarine airport** ① *20 km northwest of the city, www.melair.com.au*, has both domestic and international flights. Terminal facilities include car hire, bank ATMs, currency exchange and a **Travellers' Information Desk** ① *T9297 1805, open almost 24 hrs*, which provides accommodation and tour bookings as well as general information. From the airport, the **Skybus** ① *T9335 2811, www.skybus.com.au*, runs every 10 or 15 minutes 0355-2355 and half hourly or hourly 0025-0325 between the International terminal and the Spencer Street Coach Station (one way $16, return $26) in the city centre, also stopping near the YHAs in Abbotsford Street, North Melbourne and Courtney Street, Carlton. Tickets can be bought on board or from the information desk. A taxi between the airport and the city costs around $50.

The Bus Transit Centre, Franklin Street, is the terminal and ticket office for interstate operators **Greyhound** ① *T1300 473946, www.greyhound.com.au*. The Southern Cross Coach Station is the terminus for all services operated by **V-Line** ① *T136196, www.vline. com.au* and by **Firefly Express Coaches** ① *T1300 730740, www.fireflyexpress.com.au*, from Adelaide and Sydney.

Flinders Street Station is the main terminus for metropolitan **Metro** services, but is also the station for V-Line Gippsland services. Southern Cross Station is the main terminus for all other state **V-Line** services. All interstate trains, *The Overland*, *Ghan* (via Adelaide) and *XPT*, also operate from Southern Cross. For information on New South Wales (NSW) services refer to Great Southern Rail, www. gsr.com.au, and Cityrail, www.cityrail.com.au; for Queensland (QLD) refer to Queensland Rail, www.qr.com.au.

Getting around

All metropolitan services are operated by the Met and if intending to use public transport it's a good idea to head for the **Met Shop** ① *ground floor, Melbourne Town Hall, 103 Swanston St, Mon-Fri 0900-1700 Sat 0900-1300*. The shop has useful maps of tram, bus and train routes and timetables. For all train, bus and tram information, T131638 or refer to www.metlinkmelbourne.com.au and www.viclink.com.au.

Currently the ticketing system surrounding the Melbourne public transport system and trains, trams and buses combined has, to put it diplomatically, 'major issues'. Ask your average Melbournian commuter about it an they will laugh and shake their heads. Traditionally a single Metcard fare system covered trains, trams and buses. Three zones covered greater Melbourne, but you would rarely need anything other than a Zone 1 ticket as this covered everything within about 10 km of the city centre. The city operated a system of saver cards. Most services operated every day, from early morning to around midnight.

This system was set to change with the introduction of the new and reputedly state-of-the-art 'Myki' ticketing system in 2010. But its development and introduction was nothing short of disastrous and has been plagued with technical and financial problems. So the best current travelling advice is to consult the Visitor Information Centre or Metshop as soon as you can upon arrival for the latest details. See Transport, page 56.

Tourist information

Melbourne Visitors' Centre ① *Federation Sq, corner of Flinders St and St Kilda Rd, T03-9658 9658, www.visitmelbourne.com.au, 0900-1800*, offers information, brochures and bookings for Melbourne and the rest of the state. Also event ticketing, multilingual information and an ATM. The VIC runs one of the world's few **Greeter and Ambassador Services** ① *T9658 9658, www.thatsmelbourne.com.au/greeter*, where local volunteer 'Ambassadors' (in distinctive red attire) are staked around the city centre to offer advice, while 'Greeters' take visitors on a free sightseeing walk of the city centre. Greeters and visitors are matched by interests and language (over 30 languages spoken). There are also information booths in the Bourke Street Mall and Flinders Street Station. Melbourne has a useful telephone interpreting service, offering assistance in communication in over 100 languages, T131450 (24 hours).

City centre → *For listings, see pages 42-58.*

Melbourne has some of the best museums, galleries, gardens and architecture in the country and recent developments will ensure that the city continues to possess the most impressive spread of cultural and sporting facilities in Australia. The main tourism and urban development areas within and on the fringes of the Central Business District (CBD) are Federation Square, Southbank and Docklands. Fed Square (as it is dubbed) is the most obvious and the most celebrated. Considered a city icon, it encompasses an entire city block next to the Yarra River and Flinders Street Station. The central plaza contains space for 10,000 people, and the square buzzes with restaurants, galleries and shops. In addition, the National Gallery of Victoria on the ground floor (which is one of two major venues) highlights the importance of arts to this city. Clearly in view beyond Fed Square is the Melbourne Cricket Ground, which is another great city icon. Often referred to as the

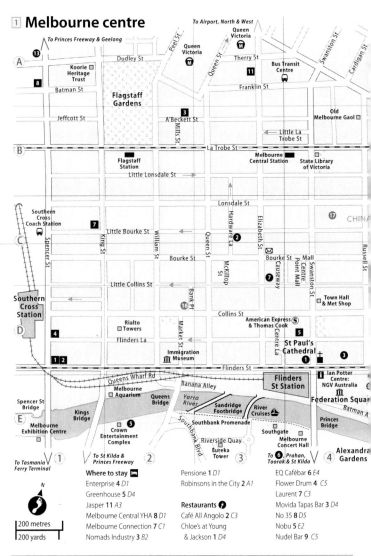

1 Melbourne centre

Where to stay 🛏
Enterprise 4 D1
Greenhouse 5 D4
Jasper 11 A3
Melbourne Central YHA 8 D1
Melbourne Connection 7 C1
Nomads Industry 3 B2
Pensione 1 D1
Robinsons in the City 2 A1

Restaurants 🍴
Café All Angolo 2 C3
Chloe's at Young
  & Jackson 1 D4
EQ Cafébar 6 E4
Flower Drum 4 C5
Laurent 7 C3
Movida Tapas Bar 3 D4
No 35 8 D5
Nobu 5 E2
Nudel Bar 9 C5

'G', it is Australia's most famous sporting venue. There is a well-developed walkway between the cricket ground and Fed square that has seen many a colourful procession over the years of both the victorious and the defeated.

Federation Square and the National Gallery of Victoria

Whether by design or location, or indeed both, Federation Square has become the main focus for visitors to Melbourne, and no matter what your movements around the city centre it always seems to draw you back. Initiated as an international architectural design competition in 1996, and finally opened in October 2002 at the mind-boggling cost of $450 million, it remains one of the most ambitious construction projects undertaken in Australia. Covering an entire block, the ultra-modern city square is an intriguing combination of angular plates, steel girders and plate glass, all cleverly housing restaurants, cafés, performance spaces, the main VIC and the supremely well-endowed **Ian Potter Centre: NGV Australia** ① T8620 2222, www.ngv.vic. gov.au, daily 1000-1700, free except for special exhibitions, which is one of two sites of the National Gallery of Victoria. This site houses the largest collection of Australian art in the world. Across the river, at 180 St Kilda Road, is the revamped **NGV International** (same details as NGV Australia), where the international collections are displayed. Especially impressive is the 19th-century European section, purchased during Melbourne's boom period.

Immigration Museum

① Old Customs House, 400 Flinders St, T131102 or T9927 2700, www.immigration. museum.vic.gov.au, 1000-1700. $8, children and concessions free.

A few blocks west of Fed Square is the late 19th-century former Customs House, which seems an appropriate spot for an immigra-

Rockpool Bar & Grill **5** E2
Rosati **11** D5
Spencer **13** A1
Victoria Arts Centre **6** B4

Bars & clubs ①
Bridie O'Reilly's **14** C5
Hairy Canary **15** C4
Mitre **16** D2
Section 8 **17** C4

City Circle Tram ▪▪▪

tion museum due to the relationship between this part of the riverbank and the city's earliest immigrants. Melbourne's culture has been heavily influenced by immigration, but this museum focuses on how the experience affected the migrants. Personal stories are told using photographs, recordings and letters, and there is even a mock ship to illustrate voyage conditions. Regular travelling exhibitions also explore the history and culture of migrants. Should you start suffering from information overload then you can always migrate to the onsite café.

Eureka Tower Skydeck
① *Riverside Quay, Southbank, T9693 8888, www.eurekalookout.com.au, daily 1000-2200, $16.50, children $9 (The Edge Experience an additional $12, children $8).*
Until mid-2006 Melbourne's tallest building was the 253-m Rialto Towers on Collins Street, but now, almost in its shadow and across the river, the Eureka Tower has surpassed it by 47 m. There is an impressive observation deck on the 88th floor. But it doesn't end there. Attached to the tower is 'The Edge', in essence, a see-through glass box that extends 3 m from the building's façade. Additional unique and impressive touches include walls that start opaque then gradually clear and soothing music that turns to the sound of grinding metal and breaking glass. There are also great views from the Sofitel Hotel, which takes up floors 35 to 50. The rooms are suitably impressive and there is also an excellent, if expensive, café and restaurant up on the 35th. If the budget doesn't allow for a sky-high meal then catch the lift up anyway for a brief glimpse, and make sure you pop to the toilet when you do.

Melbourne Aquarium
① *Yarra riverbank, T9620 0999, www.melbourneaquarium.com.au, open 0930-1800, $32, children $18.50, concessions $21.*
The Aquarium features the creatures of the Southern Ocean and offers the chance to get as close to these as most people would wish. Via a glass tunnel, visitors step into the Oceanarium, a large circular room with thick perspex walls. Sharks, stingrays, turtles and fish swim around and above you, so close that you can count the rows of teeth in the mouth of a 3-m-long shark. Several times a day divers get into the tank and feed the fish, and visitors can do the same (the sharks are kept well fed so they don't eat their tank mates). It is pricey, however: certified divers pay $150 and non-divers (who must complete a two-day resort dive course) $349. The Aquarium also has a simulated rollercoaster ride, café and shop.

Melbourne Museum and the Royal Exhibition Building
① *Carlton Gardens, 11 Nicholson St, T131102, www.melbourne.museum.vic.gov.au, 1000-1700, $8, children and concessions free.*
Due north of Fed Square is the vast and striking Melbourne Museum. Opened in 2000, it uses the most advanced display techniques to make the museum lively and interesting. Major exhibitions come and go, with some permanent features. The **Bunjilaka Aboriginal Centre** looks at the history of Aboriginal people since white invasion and the politics of displaying their possessions and artefacts. **Koorie Voices**, a photo gallery of Victorian Aboriginal people, is also fascinating for its contemporary recording of individual life stories. The **Mind and Body Gallery** examines humans in exhaustive detail, perhaps more than is palatable for the squeamish. Other highlights include the

Australia Gallery, with its focus on the social history of Melbourne and Victoria, **Bugs Alive**, with its colourful inventory of live insects and spiders, and the **Children's Gallery**, where the little darlings can check out their weight and height in 'wombats'. The museum also has an excellent shop and lots of eating choices.

Facing the Melbourne Museum, and in striking architectural contrast, is the Royal Exhibition Building, a Victorian confection built for the International Exhibition of 1880. At the time it was Australia's largest building and grand enough to be used for the opening of the first Federal Parliament. The Victorian Parliament sat here for 26 years until it was able to move back into the Victorian Parliament House (see below). The building is still used as an exhibition centre, and the museum occasionally runs tours.

Old Melbourne Gaol

ⓘ *Russell St, T9663 7228, www.nattrust.com.au, 0930-1700, $21, children $11, concessions $16.*
Near Carlton Gardens is Melbourne Gaol, built in the 1850s when Victoria was in the grip of a gold rush. Like Tasmania's Port Arthur, the design was based on the Model Prison at Pentonville in London, a system of correction that was based on isolation and silence. The three levels of cells now contain stories and death masks of female prisoners, hangmen and some of the 135 people hanged here. Visitors can also see the scaffold on which bushranger Ned Kelly was hanged in 1880, as well as his death mask and a set of Kelly Gang armour. The gaol comes alive on night tours when a tour guide acts as a prisoner from 1901 to explain the history of the gaol.

State Library of Victoria

ⓘ *328 Swanston St, corner of La Trobe St, T8664 7000, www.slv.vic.gov.au, Mon-Thu 1000-2100, Fri-Sun 1000-1800.*
Designed by Joseph Reed, who also designed the Town Hall and Exhibition Building, the doors behind the grand classical portico opened in 1856 with 3800 books chosen by the philanthropist Sir Redmond Barry. In 1913 a domed reading room was added, modelled on London's British Library and the Library of Congress in Washington. The library exhibits some of the treasures in its collection, such Audubon's *Birds of America* (the library's most valuable book) and Ned Kelly's armour. The grassy forecourt is a popular meeting place and also serves as a sculpture garden.

Koorie Heritage Trust

ⓘ *295 King St, T8622 2600, www.koorieheritagetrust.com, daily 1000-1600, donation.*
On the northwestern fringes of the CBD is the Koorie Heritage Trust. 'Koorie' is the collective name given to the Aboriginal people of southeastern Australia. The trust preserves and celebrates the 60,000 year-old history and culture of the Koorie people of Victoria from their own viewpoint. The centre has some hard-hitting history displays on the shocking results of the arrival of Europeans in 1835. There are also exhibitions of contemporary art and crafts by local Koorie people, an extensive reference library and a small shop selling some original and reproduction art.

Parliament House

ⓘ *Spring St, T9651 8568, www.parliament.vic.gov.au, tours Mon-Fri when Parliament is not sitting, 40 mins, free. Call for sitting details.*

Due south of Carlton Gardens stands the extravagant colonnaded Parliament House, at the head of a group of government buildings and the manicured parkland of the Fitzroy and Treasury Gardens (see below). It was built at the height of the gold rush in 1856 and this is reflected in its grandeur and interiors lavished with gold. Victoria's Parliament House was also the first home of the Australian Parliament after Federation in 1901. When parliament is sitting visitors can watch from the public gallery.

Fitzroy and Treasury Gardens

Some Melbournians consider these gardens the best in the city for their small scale, symmetry and avenues of European elm trees. Nearby you can find **Cook's Cottage** ⓘ *T9414 4677, 0900-1700, $5, children $2.50, concessions $3*, a tiny stone house that used to belong to Captain James Cook's family and was transported from England in 1934 to commemorate the centenary of the State of Victoria. After sunset many possums come out of the trees in Treasury Gardens and are often fed by visitors.

Melbourne Cricket Ground and the National Sports Museum

ⓘ *Jolimont St, T9657 8879, www.mcg.org.au, 0930-1630 (tours run from 1000-1500 on days without events), $15, children and concessions $11.*

For some sports fans the 'G' – as the ground is universally known – approaches the status of a temple. Built in 1853, the ground became the home of the Melbourne Cricket Club and has hosted countless historic cricket matches and Aussie Rules (Australian football) games as well as the 1956 Olympics, rock concerts and lectures. Tours of the MCG are one of Melbourne's most popular attractions and include walking into a players' changing room, stepping on to the 'hallowed turf' and visiting the members' swanky Long Room. The tour also includes entry to the National Sports Museum (Gate 3, $15, children $8) a conglomerate of the Australian Gallery of Sport, Olympic Museum, Australian Cricket Hall of Fame and exhibitions on Aussie Rules and extreme sports. Interesting highlights include Don Bradman's cricket bat, Ian Thorpe's swimming costume, Cathy Freeman's running outfit, Olympic medals and memorabilia and the original handwritten rules, drafted in 1859, of the Aussie Rules game.

Southbank

Melbourne's Southbank is the heart of the cultural and entertainment precinct. At the western end the vast, shiny **Crown Entertainment Complex** – more commonly known just as 'the casino' – includes an enormous casino, hotel, cinema, over 35 restaurants, around 20 bars and nightclubs, and boutiques. To the west, beyond the Spencer Street Bridge, is the **Melbourne Exhibition Centre**, and the new precinct redevelopment surrounding it. On the river alongside the precinct is the *Polly Woodside*, an 1885 Belfast-built iron barque, which until recent years served as the main feature of the former Melbourne Maritime Museum.

At the eastern end of Southbank, by Princes Bridge, is the **Victorian Arts Centre** ⓘ *T9281 8000, www.theartscentre.net.au, Mon-Fri 0700-late, Sat 0900-late, Sun 1000-last show*, comprising the circular Concert Hall and the Theatres Building crowned by a steel

Going for gold

Melbourne boomed during the gold rushes of the 1850s. The population exploded and the money fuelled unbelievably fast growth. By 1861 the town had founded a university, built splendid municipal buildings including a public library and museum of art, and installed street lighting, clean water and gas supplies. It couldn't last though, and at the turn of the decade banks collapsed like cards, construction ground to a halt and unemployment soared. Nearly a quarter of all Melbournians were forced to leave the city between 1891 and 1900.

The resurgence came in 1956 when the city hosted the Olympic Games, the task that finally caused it to emerge from over half a century of relative inactivity. The next couple of decades were ones of consolidation rather than flair, while by contrast its northern rival was building its famous opera house. In the 1980s Melbourne realized it was rich once more, in both finances and its diverse multi-cultural bedrock. The vibrant culture of today began to take shape and the city experienced ambition not seen for a century.

As well as attaining the title of Australia's cultural capital, aggressive state governments set out to cement its reputation as the country's sporting centre, despite Sydney landing the 2000 Olympics. With the 2006 Commonwealth Games under its belt it has not only become the nation's sporting capital but is considered by many as the sports events capital of the world, period.

Sydney and Melbourne have been notoriously competitive for decades. The simple fact is that they are quite different. Sydney wins with aesthetics and Melbourne with character. Another emerging fact is that Melbourne is set to overtake Sydney in size in the coming years and as such may one day be considered the country's 'main centre', though most Sydneysiders would scoff at the very concept.

---

net and spire. The arts centre also has free galleries, a café, quality arts shop and the city's best art and craft market, held on Sundays. It is possible to tour the complex. One of the most pleasant ways to see Southbank and the impressive border of the CBD is from the river. Many operators offer river cruises in front of Southgate; the cruises depart regularly and generally last about an hour, costing about $25.

Botanic Gardens
ⓘ *Birdwood Av, South Yarra, T9252 2300, www.rbg.vic.gov.au, Apr-Oct daily 0730-1800; Nov-Mar 0730-2030, free. Visitors' Centre Mon-Sat 0900-1700, Sat-Sun 0930-1700.*
The gardens are a large oasis just to the south of the CBD. Bordered by busy roads with the city's skyscrapers looming above, it's not easy to forget that you're in a city, but the emerald lawns, ornamental lakes and wide curving paths provide a soothing respite from crowds and concrete. The main entrance is at Observatory Gate, where there's a visitors' centre and the **Observatory Café**. A quieter and more upmarket tearoom, **The Terrace**, is by the lake. Check the Visitors' Centre for daily events, details on all the gardens' main features and in summer the outdoor theatre and cinema shows. There are several themed and specialist walking tours on offer. Consult the centre or visit the website for the latest details.

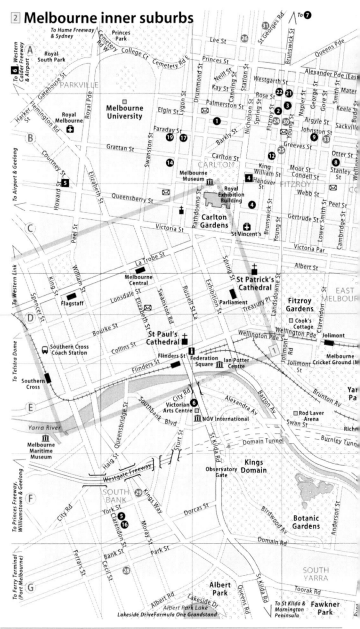

2 Melbourne inner suburbs

N

500 metres
500 yards

Where to stay 🛏
Melbourne Metro YHA **5** *B1*
Melbourne Oasis YHA **6** *A1*
Nunnery Accommodations **4** *B3*
Villa Donati **1** *E5*

Restaurants 🍴
Ablas's **1** *B3*
Babka **3** *B4*
Clarendon Fish & Chippers **5** *F2*
Cutler and Co **4** *C3*
EQ **6** *E3*
Gluttony It's a Sin **8** *B4*
Guru da Dhaba **9** *B4*
Kazen **12** *B3*
Mario's Café **2** *B3*
Moroccan Soup Bar **7** *A4*
Notturno **14** *B2*
Sakura Teppanyaki **16** *F2*
Shakahari **17** *B2*
Thresherman's Bakehouse **19** *B2*
Veggie Bar **21** *A4*
Viet Rose **22** *A3*

Bars & clubs 🍸
Bar Open **24** *B3*
Black Cat **25** *B3*
Brandon **26** *A3*
Limerick Arms **28** *G2*
Maori Chief **29** *F2*
Night Cat **30** *B4*
North Fitzroy Star **31** *A3*
Tote **33** *B4*

Inner suburbs → *For listings, see pages 42-58.*

The city centre has traditionally been thought of by visitors as the area enclosed by the circle tram, but it is far better to think of Melbourne city as a collection of inner city villages. Just to the north are Carlton, Fitzroy and Collingwood. Their proximity to the city meant that these were among the first areas to be developed as it expanded rapidly during the gold rush. **Carlton** is best known for being an area where Italian immigrants settled. It's now a middle-class area where yuppies enjoy the Italian food and cafés of Lygon Street. The neighbouring **Fitzroy** also has some fine boom-time domestic archi-tecture but had become a slum by the 1930s. Cheap rents attracted immigrants, students and artists and the area gradually gained a reputation for bohemianism. Brunswick Street is still lively and alternative although increasingly gentrified. The alternative set now claim Smith Street in **Collingwood**, just a few blocks to the east, as their own. Johnston Street, crossing Brunswick, is the centre of Melbourne's Spanish community. These areas are the liveliest of the Melbourne villages and have some of the city's best cheap eating, edgy shopping, colourful street art and raw live music venues.

Just to the west of the CBD is a vast area known as **Docklands**, as big as the CBD itself. This was the city's major port until the 1960s when containers began to be used in world shipping and vast holding sheds were no longer needed. The area has undergone some massive redevelopment in the last 10 years or so, transforming the area into an attractive waterfront precinct for inner city offices, apartments, restaurants, shops and enter-tainment venues. The flagship is the Etihad Stadium, a major venue for Aussie Rules football matches and Rugby League games. It is a great venue for a walk and views across the CBD.

Southeast of the centre, **Richmond** is the place to come for Vietnamese cuisine and offers the inner city's best range of factory outlet shopping on Bridge Road and Swan Street. Greeks populated the suburb before the Vietnamese and the community is still represented in the restaurants of Swan Street. South of the river, **Toorak** and **South Yarra** have long been the most exclusive residential suburbs and this is mirrored in the quality of the shops and cafés at the northern end of Chapel Street. The southern end becomes funkier and less posh as it hits **Prahran**, where Greville Street is full of second-hand clothes shops, bookshops and cafés and Commercial Street is the centre of the city's gay community. These suburbs are among the most fashionable and stylish and unsurprisingly Chapel Street is a wonderful destination for clothes shopping.

Down by the bay **St Kilda** has a charm all of its own. An early seaside resort that became seedy and run down, it's now a cosmopolitan and lively suburb but still has an edge. Only the well-heeled can afford to buy here and though some of them aren't too keen on living next to the junkies and prostitutes still seen on Grey Street, the picturesque foreshore makes this the most relaxed of the inner suburbs and a great place to base oneself for a few days. Here also is **Luna Park** ⓘ *Cavell St, T9534 5764, www.lunapark.com.au, mid-Apr until mid-Sep Sat-Sun 1100-1800 and mid-Sep until mid-Apr Fri 1900-2300, Sat 1100-2300, Sun 1100-1800, from $35.95, children $25.95 and family $123*, a fairground with some impressive rides and an unmistakable front door.

The rural area northeast of Melbourne is promoted as a Valley of the Arts for its past and present links with artists' communities. A path winds along the Yarra River from the city centre to **Eltham** (25 km) so hiring a bicycle is a good way to explore these leafy and tranquil areas beyond the city. An important stop along the way is the **Heide Museum of Modern Art** ⓘ *7 Templestowe Rd, Bulleen, signposted from Eastern Freeway, T9850 1500, www.heide.com.au, Tue-Fri 0900-1700, Sat-Sun 1200-1700, $12, children free, concessions $8*, the former home of art patrons John and Sunday Reed during the 1930s and 1940s. The museum is set in beautiful bushland by the river and includes a sculpture garden with works by Anish Kapoor and Anthony Caro. The gallery has an exceptional collection of modern Australian art and hosts temporary exhibitions of contemporary art.

If you have your own transport and want to see something unique and Australian, head to the Bellbird Picnic Area (off Yarra Boulevard, location Melway 2D K6). You'll see a vast array of bizarre Christmas tree decorations there, as well as the largest **Flying Fox (fruit bat) colony** in Victoria.

Around Melbourne → *For listings, see pages 42-58.*

There is great variety of scenery and many activities around Melbourne, so even if you are short of time you can still see something of the state's attractions within a day. The Yarra Valley is a beautiful wine region with some of the most sophisticated cellar doors and accompanying restaurants in Australia. Nearby, Healesville has a wonderful wildlife sanctuary, and just beyond there is a very scenic winding drive through forest and ferns on the way to Marysville. The once beautiful sub-Alpine village of Marysville was effectively razed during the 'Black Saturday' bush fires of February 2009, with the loss of 47 lives and almost all man-made structures. Although the bush is regenerating, little remains of the village itself and until it is rebuilt it is a sad testament to the devastation that bush fires can cause. Local natural sights still worth seeing include the 84-m Steavenson Falls (4 km from Marysville).

Heading south, the Dandenongs is a fine area in which to walk or drive through towering mountain ash forests, and if you're lucky you might just see an elusive lyrebird. The Mornington Peninsula, often just called 'the bay', has some great beaches as well as diving or swimming with dolphin trips, and the penguins of Phillip Island are among the region's most popular attractions.

Getting there and around

Mornington Peninsula VIC ⓘ *Point Nepean Rd, Dromana, T5987 3078, www.visitmornington peninsula.org, 0900-1700*. **Phillip Island VIC** ⓘ *1 km past the bridge on Phillip Island Tourist Rd, T5956 7447, www.visitphillipisland.com, open 0900-1700*, has a great range of local information. **Phillip Island Nature Park** ⓘ *T5951 2800, www.penguins.org.au*, manages most of the wildlife attractions. Saver tickets (the Nature Park Pass) can be bought at the VIC. **Dandenongs VIC** ⓘ *Burwood Highway, Upper Fern Tree Gully, T9758 7522, www.yarravalley tourism.com, 0900-1700*. They sell the Parks Victoria walking map for $2. **Yarra Valley VIC** ⓘ *The Old Courthouse, Harker St, Healesville, T5962 2600, www.visityarravalley.com.au, www.yarravalleytourism.asn.au*.

Mornington Peninsula

This is Melbourne's beach playground, where you can swim with dolphins, dive and sail, visit some world-class vineyards, play some of Australia's best golf courses, or take a trip to French and Phillip Islands. Both the peninsula's popularity and its proximity to Melbourne have resulted in a suburban sprawl creeping down as far as Rye, but beyond this things improve dramatically. The pristine south coast is protected by the Mornington Peninsula National Park; and the beaches and cafés of Sorrento and Portsea can make for a memorable stay.

Just east of the coastal suburb of Dromana is **Arthur's Seat**, a 300-m-high hill in Arthur's Seat State Park with striking views over Port Phillip Bay. At the top there are some pleasant, easy walks in the state park, as well as the Seawinds Botanic Gardens and a maze.

Near the tip of Mornington's curving arm is **Sorrento**, its shore lined with jetties, boats and the odd brightly coloured bathing box. The town has been popular for seaside holidays since the 1880s and consequently has many fine old limestone buildings along the main street, Ocean Beach Road. The Back Beach at Sorrento is also one of the best in the state with everything from views to rock pools ideal for snorkelling. A few kilometres further on is **Portsea**, a small suburb frequented by wealthy Melbournians and boasting the stunning Portsea Back Beach. Both Sorrento and Portsea are full of stylish cafés, pubs and shops. **Point Nepean** is the long, thin tip of the Mornington Peninsula, where it's possible to explore the gun emplacements, tunnels and bunkers of **Fort Nepean** ⓘ *T5984 4276, 0900-1700, $8.10, children $3.90*. From the Visitors' Centre there is a short drive to Gunners car park; from here you can walk to the fort, about 3.5 km, with magnificent views over Bass Strait and the Bay, or you can take the visitors' bus ($17, children $10).

This long, straight strip of **Mornington Peninsula National Park** stretches from Portsea down to Cape Schank, protecting the last bit of coastal tea tree on the peninsula and the spectacular sea cliffs from the golden limestone at Portsea to the brooding black basalt around Cape Schank. There are picnic areas and a lighthouse at the cape and some good walks. There are also regular tours of the light station, and the lighthouse keepers' cottages have been renovated for holiday letting. There is a short walk with excellent views from the Cape Schank car park out to the end of the cape. For a longer walk,

Bushrangers Bay Track is a great coastal route along the cliffs to the sublime and picturesque Bushranger Bay, ending at Main Creek (45 minutes one way).

The Mornington Peninsula is also well known for its world-class **vineyards**. Mornington wine production dates back to 1886 but was not begun in earnest until the

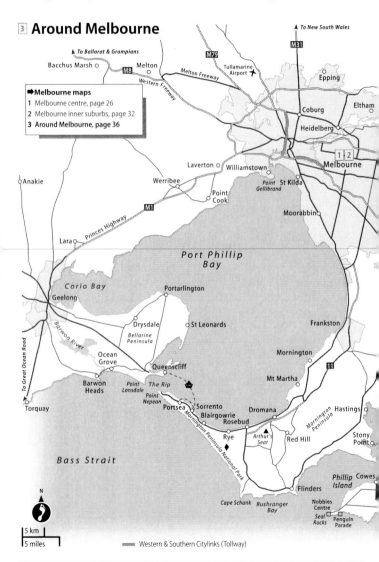

3 Around Melbourne

➡**Melbourne maps**
1 Melbourne centre, page 26
2 Melbourne inner suburbs, page 32
3 Around Melbourne, page 36

▲ *To New South Wales*

▲ *To Ballart & Grampians*

Bacchus Marsh ○

M8 Melton ○
Melton Freeway
Western Freeway

M79 Tullamarine Airport ✈

Epping

Coburg
Heidelberg
Eltham

Melbourne 1 2

Laverton ○ Williamstown

Werribee

Point Cook

Point St Kilda
Gellibrand

Moorabbin ○

○ Anakie

Princes Highway M1

Lara ○

Port Phillip Bay

Corio Bay

Geelong

Portarlington

Drysdale ○ St Leonards

Bellarine Peninsula

Frankston

Ocean Grove

Queenscliff

Mornington ○

Mt Martha ○

Barwon Heads

Point Lonsdale *The Rip*

Point Nepean Portsea ○ Sorrento
Blairgowrie
Rosebud

Dromana

11

Mornington Peninsula

Hastings ○

Stony Point ○

To Great Ocean Road

Barwon River

Torquay ○

Bass Strait

Rye

Arthur's Seat ▲

Red Hill

Mornington Peninsula National Park

Phillip Island

Cowes ○

Flinders ○

Cape Schank *Bushranger Bay*

Nobbies Centre □
Seal Rocks ○ Penguin Parade □

N

5 km
5 miles

═══ Western & Southern Citylinks (Tollway)

early 1970s. The region is recognized as the home of Australian Pinot Noir, with around 200 vineyards and 50 cellar doors, many with quality restaurants or cafés attached. If you're short of time, don't miss what is arguably the most lauded of all the peninsula's vineyards, **Montalto** ⓘ *33 Shoreham Rd, Red Hill, T5989 8412, www.montalto.com.au*. The VIC in Dromana can provide full details and tour options.

Peninsula Hot Springs ⓘ *Springs Lane, T5950 8777, ww.peninsulahotsprings.com, daily 0730-2200, from$30*, is one of the most popular and unexpected attractions on the peninsula. Located in a peaceful bush setting just south of Rye, the 17-ha complex hosts a range of indoor and outdoor pools, a day spa and a café. Recommended.

Phillip Island

Phillip Island is one of Victoria's biggest attractions, with 3.5 million visitors a year. Connected to the mainland by a bridge, the island is 26 km long and 9 km wide. It certainly has its natural attractions, such as the rocky coves and headlands in the south and sunny north-facing beaches around Cowes, but the island has long since been tamed. Some wildlife continues to thrive, however, and this has been the lynchpin of the island's tourism success, particularly the rather overrated Penguin Parade. Other visitors come for the superb surfing breaks along the dangerous south coast and the safe swimming beaches on the sandy northern shores. There are some pleasant walking tracks throughout the island, particularly on **Cape Woolamai**. **Newhaven**, by the bridge, and **Cowes** are the main towns, while **Rhyll** has a quiet charm away from the crowds. **San Remo** is the gateway town, with accommodation a shade cheaper than on the island itself. The **Australian Motorcycle Grand Prix** is held here.

At the far end of the island are the **Nobbies**, a series of rocky islands joined to the coast at low tide, and beyond them **Seal Rocks**, home to Australia's largest fur seal colony. There is a new state-of-the-art visitors' centre and a series of boardwalks weave their way down past through penguin

habitats to the rock shelf below. The seals can only be seen with powerful binoculars and a live webcam in the centre, but fairy penguins and gulls can often be seen sheltering under the boardwalks. The road out there is closed at dusk, when the **Penguin Parade** ① *visitor centre, T5951 2800, www.penguins.org.au, from 1000, parade from dusk, $21.20, children $10.60, concessions $14.80*, gets into gear. Fairy penguins burrow in their thousands in the dunes along this stretch of coast, coming ashore in the darkness after a hard day at sea. Huge grandstands and powerful lights have been erected to allow thousands of visitors to watch the tired birds struggle out of the water and up the beach. Koalas are best seen at the **Koala Conservation Centre** ① *Phillip Island Rd, 1000-1700, $10.60, children $5.30, concessions $7.40*, via an excellent series of elevated boardwalks through stands of gum trees. Other spots include **Swan Lake**, the island's only freshwater lake near Penguin Parade, **Cape Woolamai**, with its popular and pleasant walking tracks, and **Rhyll Inlet**, a wetland habitat favoured by migratory wading birds. Swan Lake and Rhyll both have boardwalks and bird hides.

Dandenong Ranges

Also referred to as the 'Dandenongs' or simply 'the mountain', these ranges comprise a hilly forested massif just to the east of Melbourne. They are a very popular destination for daytrippers, who swamp some parts at weekends and during school holidays. Several loosely connected chunks have been designated the **Dandenong Ranges National Park** ① *$2.20 per car, entry before 1600*, and are crisscrossed with some wonderful walking tracks. Great views can be had from several points, the best over Melbourne being from the summit of Mount Dandenong itself. At the base of the mountain are the service towns of Fern Tree Gully and Belgrave. At the latter is the station for **Puffing Billy** ① *T9757 0700, www.puffingbilly.com.au, from 1030, $35, children $17.50* (return), the popular picturesque steam train that winds its way through scenic hilly country east to Gembrook, 24 km away. On the mountain itself **Sassafras** is the largest and most popular town, with a good range of facilities.

There are hundreds of interconnecting walking trails, and it is possible to organize circular walks from 10 minutes to three days in length, though longer walks may require short stretches on vehicular roads, and there is no camping on the mountain. Grants Picnic Grounds, just south of Kallista, is often inundated with cockatoos and crimson rosellas all keen to share your lunch and also serves as the start of several good loop tracks that pass through spectacular mountain ash forests and fern gullies. Lyrebirds live in these forests but are far more shy and difficult to spot than their assorted and cheeky pscittacine cousins. For an excellent circular walk through their territory, park at Cook's Corner and head down the Lyrebird Walk (7 km, two hours).

Yarra Valley and around

The Yarra Valley is one of Victoria's best known and most visited wine districts, but not content with creating great wine some of the wineries here have restaurants of the highest standard, and dining rooms and terraces that rank amongst the most striking and scenic in the country. In summer the valley gets very busy, particularly at weekends. Just east of the valley is another excellent reason to visit – Healesville Sanctuary, the best native wildlife park of its kind in Australia.

There are 40-plus wineries in the valley, most of which offer food. This is just a sample. **Rochford-Eyton** ① *Maroondah Highway, T5962 2119, www.rochford wines.com, wines $20-50, cellar door daily 1000-1700, lunches 1200-1500*, is striking for its modern architecture and has a fine dining room overlooking a lake. The excellent Merlot and the expensive modern Australian cuisine are regarded by many as the best in the valley. In summer, outdoor classical concerts add to the experience. At **Yering Station** ① *38 Melba Highway, T9730 0100, www.yering.com, wines $15-50, cellar door 1000-1700, lunches daily*, tastings and Yarra Valley produce are held in an old farm building, but don't miss a stroll around the new restaurant and cellars. This graceful sweep of stone and glass has the feel of a Bond movie, and the massive terrace has huge views. **McWilliam's Lilydale** ① *Davross Court, T5964 2016, wines $20-25, cellar door daily 1100-1700, flexible lunch hours*, is a small and very friendly winery with an octagonal conservatory dining room and vine-hung garden gazebo, both looking out over vines and gum woods. There are simple cheap platters and cook-it-yourself barbecue meals. The salad bar is balanced by the scrumptious puddings. **Domaine Chandon** ① *Maroondah Highway, T9739 1110, wines $25-50, cellar door daily 1030-1630*, is part of the Möet group, with a stylish but relaxed tasting room with a high arched window looking out over the valley. A small savoury platter is served with each $5-10 glass of bubbly. A couple are good for a snack lunch. There are no free tastings. Finally, **Long Gully** ① *Long Gully Rd, T9510 5798, wines $15-30, cellar door daily 1100-1700*, is a small easy-going winery with a very picturesque setting in its own mini-valley, making excellent and good value wines. Picnickers are welcome on the cellar door balcony.

Healesville Sanctuary ① *T5957 2800, www.zoo.org.au, 0900-1700, $25, children $13, concessions $18.50. A few buses daily from corner of Green St and Maroondah Highway, Healesville, Mon-Fri from 0925, Sat 0858, Sun 1133*, 4 km from the little town of Healesville, on Badger Creek Road, is devoted to the conservation, breeding and research of Australian wildlife. The appeal of this place is seeing animals being so well cared for, including species that are almost impossible to see in the wild, including Tasmanian devils, platypus, the endangered orange-bellied parrot, the lyrebird and Leadbeater's possum. The sanctuary has 30 ha of bushland with Badger Creek running through its centre. Visitors walk along a wide circular path (1.5 km), taking side loops to see the creatures that interest them. Highlights are the Animal Close-Up sessions, held several times a day, when you can get as close as is legally allowed to wombats and koalas. The star exhibit is the World of the Platypus, a nocturnal tunnel with glass windows where you can watch the little fellas swimming and hunting. The most recent addition to the zoo is the Australian Wildlife Health Centre. An impressive multi-million dollar facility, it cares for sick or injured native wildlife from all over Victoria and offers the visitor a unique live view of the working veterinary hospital.

Great Ocean Road → *For listings, see pages 42-58.*

The three great natural attractions of Australia are often said to be 'the road, the rock and the reef'. The 'road' is the Great Ocean Road, which runs west from Anglesea, round the treacherous Cape Otway, to Warrnambool. It is truly one of the great coastal routes of the world and has everything, from stylish villages such as Lorne and Apollo Bay, backed by a lush hinterland of forests and waterfalls inhabited by glow worms and platypuses, to Port

Campbell National Park, whose famous golden rock stacks are seared into the minds of most travellers long before they see them for real.

Getting there and around
Getting around The road is congested all year, but especially in summer, when there is a procession of slow coaches. If you can, plan a route from west to east to avoid it all. Most traffic and tours travel west from Melbourne along the Great Ocean Road, then return eastwards to the city along the faster inland route, the Princes Highway. There are V-Line bus services along the Great Ocean Road to Warrnambool from Geelong, which stop regularly along the way. Backpacker buses from Melbourne also have a Great Ocean Road service (see page 56) and there are daily V-Line direct train services from Geelong to Warrnambool (two hours and 20 minutes).

Tourist information The **VIC** ① *Princes Highway, Little River, north of Geelong, T1800 620888, www.greatoceanroad.org.au, 0900-1700*, is for the whole region, from Geelong to Port Fairy. There are also numerous VICs en route including Torquay, Beach Road, T1300 614219; Apollo Bay, 100 Great Ocean Road, T5237 6529, and Warrnambool, Merri Street, T1800 637725.

The route
Start off at **Lorne**, a glamorous coastal town of classy boutiques and fine restaurants surrounded by the thick forest, rivers and waterfalls of Angahook-Lorne State Park. Next up is **Apollo Bay**, a relaxed and friendly town and a good base from which to explore the **Otway National Park**, just to the west. Among the highlights of Otway National Park is Maits Rest Rainforest Walk. The towering mountain ash surrounding the upper edges of the gully are also impressive. Koala, swamp wallabies and yellow-bellied gliders live in the park, along with the rare spot-tailed quoll. The best place to see koala is in the roadside bush around the turn-off (left) to Blanket Bay Campsite, which in turn is along the main road to the Otway Lightstation.

West of the cape the sheer limestone cliffs have been eroded into a series of huge rock stacks, sculpted by the elements themselves into a series of arches, caves and tapering sails. The most famous group of stacks, the **Twelve Apostles**, was dramatically reduced to 11 when one of the stacks collapsed into the sea in June 2005, an event witnessed by a group of tourists (minus video camera, unfortunately). The most fascinating area of this stretch of the road is beautiful Loch Ard Gorge, named after the ship that was wrecked on Mutton Bird Island in 1878, killing 52 people on board. There is a walk from a lookout over the wreck site to the gorge and beach and then to the cemetery.

Beyond Port Campbell are more rock features, The Arch, London Bridge and The Grotto. The latter is probably the most interesting but London Bridge is famous for losing the arch connecting it to the mainland in 1990 and leaving some astonished tourists stranded on the far side. Adjoining Port Campbell, beyond the tiny settlement of Peterborough, is the Bay of Islands Coastal Park, an area of countless striking rock stacks. At Warrnambool the Great Ocean Road meets the Princes Highway. Only a stone's throw from here is the long, curving Lady Bay, with some of the coast's best swimming and boogie-boarding beaches, and the rugged low headlands and tiny bays that stretch away from the breakwater at its western end. The Thunder Point Coastal Walk runs along the top of these cliffs and at low tide offers the opportunity to wade out to Middle Island, with its rocky outcrops, caves and small fairy-penguin rookery. Just to the east of the town, across Hopkins River, there is a very good opportunity for seeing southern right whales from the free viewing platforms at Logans Beach (between mid-July and mid-September).

If you have the time, want to shed a few kilos and get really intimate with the coastline (and the odd koala) then consider doing the new Great Ocean Walk. Considered Victoria's premiere walking track, it stretches 104 km from Apollo Bay in the east to The Twelve Apostles. It can be tackled in whole or in part with a wide range of accommodation choices along the way, from luxury B&Bs to remote beachside campsites. For more information, consult Parks Victoria, the local Visitor Information Centres and the dedicated website.

◉ Melbourne and around listings

For Where to stay and Restaurant price codes and other relevant information, see pages 13-17.

⊜ Where to stay

Melbourne has a huge range of places to stay. The centre is first choice for most visitors, put off by the term 'suburbs', but the suburbs are only a 10-min walk away, boast an equally buzzing café society and nightlife and also offer better value and, in peak times, more choice. Most places are priced at a year-round rate, though some hostels will be cheaper in winter. St Kilda is something of a backpacking stronghold, though be aware that the quality of accommodation varies considerably. Almost everyone hikes their prices up for big events: the Melbourne Cup, Australian Open, Grand Prix and AFL Grand Final.

City centre *p25, map p26*
$$$$ Robinsons in the City, 405 Spencer St, T9329 2552, www.robinsonsinthecity. com.au. A quality 4-star 6-bedroom boutique B&B in a former 1850s bakery. Contemporary decor, queen or king suites. Parking available with pre-booking.
$$$$-$$$ Jasper, 489 Elizabeth St, T8327 2777, www.jasperhotel.com.au. Newly renovated and very slick. Good-value double, twin and 2-bedroom suites. Pool, cable TV and Wi-Fi. Light or cooked breakfasts from $20. Discounted parking.
$$$ Pensione Hotel, 16 Spencer St, T9621 3333, www.pensione.com.au. Recently fully renovated and good value mid-range hotel.
$$$-$$ Enterprise, 44 Spencer St, T9629 6991, www.hotelenterprise.com.au. A modest contemporary chain hotel with good value en suite doubles, but sadly, no Captain Kirk, Scotty or beaming up from foyer to room. Undercover parking $25 per night.
$$ Nomads Industry, 198 A'Beckett St, T9328 4863, www.nomadsindustry.com. Modern and well-managed 'flashpackers'

considered one of the best in the city. Relatively spacious doubles, some en suite and a female-only wing. Quality facilities include a cinema lounge, rooftop deck, bar and internet lounge. Recommended.
$$-$ Greenhouse, 228 Flinders Lane, T9639 6400, greenhouse@friendlygroup.com.au, and **$$-$ Hotel Bakpak**, 167 Franklin St, T9329 7525, www.bakpak group.com. Each has around 200 beds and a distinctly corporate feel, so these backpacker hostels are not a home-from-home, but both are modern, clean with good facilities and lots of organized events. Some doubles with en suite. Linen, pick-ups, free internet.
$$-$ Melbourne Central YHA, 562 Flinders St, www.yha.com.au. Newly renovated, 208-bed, 5-storey, heritage-listed building is ideally located in the Melbourne CBD and overlooks the North Shore of the Yarra. It has all the usual excellent modern YHA facilities and attention to detail, plus a few special features like rooftop terrace and funky ground-floor bar.
$$-$ Melbourne Connection, 205 King St, T9642 4464, www.melbourneconnection.com. One of the smaller city-centre hostels with around 80 beds, including simple but pleasant doubles, stripped wood floors and comfortable communal facilities (though the kitchen could be bigger). Usual facilities including satellite TV and Wi-Fi. Friendly and helpful owners also give the place a good atmosphere.

North of the centre *p33, map p32*
$$$-$ Nunnery Accommodations, 116 Nicholson St, T9419 8637, www.nunnery. com.au. Friendly, funky backpacker hostel in a rambling Victorian terraced house with a seriously comfortable front lounge. Free linen, breakfast and lots of laid-on activities. Range of doubles, twins, 3-beds and cheaper 12-bed dorms. There is also boutique accommodation available in newly refurbished premises in Fitzroy.

$$-$ Melbourne Metro YHA, 78 Howard St, T9329 8427, www.yha.com.au. Purpose-built, 350-bed hostel with mostly 4-bed dorms, doubles and twins, some en suite. All the usual YHA facilities, free use of bikes and car parking.

$$-$ Melbourne Oasis YHA, 76 Chapman St, T9328 3595, www.yha.com.au. This smaller, homely, backpackers has 120 beds, all in 4-bed dorms or smaller, good-value doubles. Modern and comfortable with a gazebo and garden, free bike hire and parking.

Southeast of the centre p33

$$$$ The Prince, 2 Acland St, St Kilda, T9536 1111, www.theprince.com.au. Sleek boutique hotel, the height of hushed minimalist luxury with its own spa (see page 54). The 40 en suite rooms are seriously stylish and the pool and deck one of the city's finest posing spots. The smart fine dining restaurant, **Circa**, offers a business lunch for around $30. The basement **Mink** bar plays the tune to an Eastern bloc theme with leather couches and more varieties of vodka than a Russian distiller on speed.

$$$$-$$$ Villa Donati, 377 Church St, T9428 8104, www.villadonati.com. Charming and good value 4½-star boutique hotel located 2.5 km from the city centre. Chic, classy rooms with a mix of European and Asian furnishings. Fine café-style breakfast. On-street parking.

$$$-$ Claremont, 189 Toorak Rd, Toorak, T9826 8000, www.hotelclaremont.com. Bottom end of the category, it has clean, bright but sparse rooms of good value and also 12 serviced apartments nearby. Mostly singles, doubles and twins. Linen, substantial continental breakfast, use of kitchenette.

$$ Olembia, 96 Barkly St, St Kilda, T9537 1412, www.olembia.com.au. Very comfortable and carefully planned hostel. 50 beds, including a dozen doubles and twins with shared bathroom facilities. Very competent, friendly and knowledgeable management create the classic homely

environment. Bike hire, free off-street parking and secure bike shed.

$$-$ Base Backpackers, 17 Carlisle St, St Kilda, T8598 6200, www.baseback packers.com. Hip and modern and part of the expanding Australasian chain. Women-only floor boasting hair straighteners, make-up boxes etc! Red laminate floors, futon-style beds, in-house bar, fast internet.

$$-$ Chapel St Backpackers, 22 Chapel St, Prahran, T9533 6855, www.csbackpackers.com.au. Right at the bottom of this street is this friendly, family-run hostel with 48 beds. Mostly doubles, twins and 4-bed dorms, some women only. Almost all are en suite with a/c, modest facilities. Linen and breakfast included.

$$-$ Habitat HQ St Kilda, 333 St Kilda Rd, St Kilda, T9537 3777, www.thehabitathq.com.au. Large, modern and well-facilitated place just a short stroll from the beach and those cake shops on Acland St. Usual room configurations from doubles (some en suite with TV) to 10-bed dorms. Car parking, cable TV, airport pick-ups.

$$-$ The Pint on Punt, 42 Punt St, St Kilda, T9510 4273, www.pintonpunt.com.au. Irish-style pub with good hostel accommodation upstairs. See also page 43.

Mornington Peninsula p35

$$$$-$$ Oceanic Whitehall, 231 Ocean Beach Rd, Sorrento, T5984 4166, www.oceanic group.com.au. A grand old limestone guesthouse, traditional rooms with shared facilities, also some rooms with en suite, spa, open fire. Only a short stroll from Sorrento Back Beach, one of the best on the peninsula.

$$ Bayplay Adventure Lodge, 46 Canterbury Jetty Rd, Blairgowrie, T5984 0888, www.bayplay.com.au. Good hostel run by dive operators (see page 55), with rooms, dorms, pool and café. Also offers transfers to and from Melbourne. There is also a self-contained cottage (**$$$**) sleeping 4-6 at St Andrews Beach.

$$ Lighthouse keepers' cottages, Cape Schank, T5988 6184, capeschank@austpac inns.com.au. These have been renovated for holiday letting and can be booked by the room or as a whole.

$$ Sorrento YHA, 3 Miranda St, Sorrento, T5984 4323, www.yha.com.au. Small, clean and very friendly hostel, owners help with arranging work (Apr-Jul) in local wineries and with tours and transport.

Phillip Island *p37*
Most of the accommodation for casual visitors is in Cowes, though there are a few options elsewhere on the island. There are dozens of motels and cheaper caravan parks. Most get booked out for long weekends and school holidays. Reserve a bed early.

$$$$-$$$ Cliff Top Boutique Accommodation, 1 Marlin St, T5952 1033, www.clifftop.com.au. Secluded 1.2-ha oceanfront property with seven luxury rooms, some with spa. Regarded as one of the best establishments on the island. Recommended.

$$$$-$$ Big 4 Phillip Island Caravan Park, 24 Beach Crescent, Newhaven, T5956 7227, www.big4.com.au. Motor park with good facilities handy for the visitors' information centre, San Remo shops and the beautiful Cape Woolamai.

$$ Beach Park Tourist Caravan Park, 2 McKenzie Rd, T5952 2113. Wide range of sites, cabins and units and camp kitchen.

$$-$ Amaroo Park YHA, 97 Church St, T5952 2548, www.yha.com.au. Of the 2 excellent and friendly backpacker hostels, this is by far the larger, with more facilities, very cheap breakfast and dinner (available to non-residents), a bar and pool. It also operates the Duck Truck and offers free transportation from Melbourne.

Dandenong Ranges *p38*
There are over 100 B&Bs on the mountain itself, with most catering for the high-end 4-poster open fire market. There are surprisingly no hostels or caravan parks and no camping facilities, though there are a couple of cheaper motels along Burwood Highway.

$$$$ Glen Harrow, Old Monbulk Rd, Belgrave, Dandenong Ranges, T9754 3232, www.glenharrow.com.au. Oozing character, it has 4 exquisite old gardeners' cottages, set in 8 ha of wild gardens. Completely self-contained and furnished mostly with antiques.

$$$$-$$$ Como Cottages, 1465 Mount Dandenong Tourist Rd, Olinda, T9751 2264, www.comocottages.com. A range of charming 1-3 bedroom self-contained cottages. The 4-poster, the fire and the spa are all at affordable mid-week prices. Go on – spoil yourselves.

Yarra Valley and around *p38*
The valley is awash with boutique hotel and B&B accommodation. Budget options are very thin on the ground, but there are a couple in Healesville.

$$$ Art at Linden Gate, 899 Healesville Yarra Glen Rd, T9730 1861, erfrics@netstra.com.au. Single self-contained B&B apartment, with limited kitchen facilities, in the mud-brick house of a local sculptor. Isolated grounds encompass a hobby vineyard and a tiny wine cellar. The upstairs gallery has a range of contemporary work.

$$$ Strathvea B&B, 755 Myers Creek Rd, T5962 4109, www.strathvea.com.au. Gracious 11-room B&B in its own wooded clearing adjacent to the state forest. Shared bathroom or en suite rooms. Fine cooked breakfast. Lots of wildlife and walking tracks nearby.

$$ Healesville Hotel, 256 Maroondah Highway, Healesville, T5962 4002, www.healesvillehotel.com.au. This pub has 7 funky, spacious and brightly coloured rooms upstairs with shared facilities and a good bistro with great country cooking (mid-range). Meals Thu-Mon 1200-1430, daily 1800-2030. Book ahead for rooms at weekends.

Great Ocean Road *p39*

Accommodation is very expensive in high season but Apollo Bay has a couple of gems.

$$$$ Queenscliff, 16 Gellibrand St, Queenscliff, T5258 1066, www.queenscliff hotel.com.au. At the southeasterly tip of the Bellarine Peninsula, southeast from Geelong, is the graceful, genteel Edwardian seaside resort of Queenscliff. One of the grandest hotels in town, and a real window into Edwardian decadence, is this beautifully restored place. Not only is it a most sumptuous place to stay but the high standards are also reflected in what comes out of the kitchens. Lunches in the shop café, also bar meals, bistro and a separate dining room.

$$$$-$$$ Cape Otway Lighthouse, T5237 9240, www.lightstation.com. For something a bit different check out this large residence in the old keeper's cottage. It has 4 comfortable bedrooms and lounges with sofas and open fires, as well as the incredible position. Also 2 cheaper studio rooms for couples.

$$$ Angel's Guesthouse, 7 Campbell Court, T5237 7085, www.angelasguesthouse. com.au. Spacious rooms with cheerful linen, spotless bathrooms and balconies. Angela's provides the warmest hospitality imaginable and the rooms are good value.

Restaurants

Melbourne is foodie heaven. It boasts an incredible variety at inexpensive prices. In fact, the choice of restaurants can be overwhelming. A quarter of all Melbournians were born outside Australia and there are roughly 110 ethnic groups living in the city who have enriched Melbourne cuisine. Such is the breadth and quality of cuisine that the city can now claim to be ahead of Sydney – much to the latter's chagrin. The best option is to head for an 'eat street' or area known for a particular cuisine, such as Brunswick St in Fitzroy or the Vietnamese restaurants of Richmond, and stroll up and down to see

what appeals. During the day look out for the Mon-Fri business lunches at some of the fancier restaurants: starter, main course and glass of wine for $25-35. Despite the vast number of seats, try to book in summer and at weekends.

City centre *p25, map p26*

City centre eating tends to be lunch-based. For greater choice in the evening most people head for the inner suburbs, although Chinatown (Little Bourke St) and the Southbank remain busy dinner spots. There are cheaper options on Russell St. Hardware Lane, to the west of Elizabeth St, has a strip of restaurants and cafés that buzz at lunchtimes. Centre Lane, off Collins St, at first glance looks like a grimy dark alley but is one of the best places in the city centre for a cheap lunch.

$$$ Flower Drum, 17 Market Lane, T9662 3655, www.flower-drum.com. Mon-Sat 1200-1500, 1800-2300, Sun 1800-2230. Considered by many to be the best Chinese restaurant in Australia and well worth the painful hit to the wallet. The finest Cantonese cuisine in a light, elegant dining room, impeccable service and an excellent wine list. The Peking duck must be tried. Expect to spend about $150 for 2 without wine. Recommended.

$$$ Nobu, Crown Complex, 8 Whiteman St, Southbank, T9292 7879, www.nobu restaurants.com. Lunch Mon-Thu 1200-1430, Fri-Sun 1200-1500; dinner Sun-Thu 1800-2230, Fri-Sat 1800-2300. Bar menu daily from 1730. Opened amid much hype and in partnership with actor Robert de Niro, the Nobu chain of classy Japanese restaurants has now arrived down under. The fact Melbourne was chosen over Sydney caused quite a stir – quite literally.

$$$ Rockpool Bar and Grill, Crown Complex, Southbank, T8648 1900, www.rockpool melbourne.com. Sun-Fri 1200-1500, daily for dinner Sat. Multi award-winner and sister to the famous

Sydney establishment. Home of lauded chef Neil Perry who is renowned for 'turning great produce into something memorable'. Steak is a house speciality.

$$ EQ Cafébar, Victorian Arts Centre, Riverside Terr, 100 St Kilda Rd, T9645 0644. Mon-Sat 1100-late. A little further south of the centre, for good casual Mediterranean food in a combined bar and café. Noisy but lively contemporary space.

$$ No 35, Level 35, Sofitel Hotel, 25 Collins St, T9653 7744. Daily from 0630-late. Ideal opportunity to get above the city mayhem and take in some great views. Modern à la carte Australian cuisine. Their buffet breakfasts are expensive but worth it.

$$ Rosati, 95 Flinders La, T9654 7772, www.rosati.com.au. Mon-Fri 0730-2200, Sat 1800-2200. Large, light Italian café-bar in an old glass-ceilinged warehouse that the owners have succeeded in giving a welcoming, classical feel.

$$ Sakura Teppanyaki, 331 Clarendon St, South Bank, T9699 4150. Mon-Fri 1100-1500, daily 1700-2300, later Fri-Sat. Leaving the centre southwards, the chefs throw their lively personalities into their cooking, and things can get pretty boisterous here. Good fun.

$$-$ Chloe's Lounge at Young and Jackson, upstairs, corner Swanston St and Flinders St, T9650 3884, www.youngand jacksons.com.au. Lunch daily 1200-1430; dinner Sun-Thu 1730-2100, Fri-Sat 1730-2130. Very conveniently located and quiet sanctuary amid the city chaos, above one of the city's best-known traditional pubs. Tapas for lunch and a quality full dinner menu. Arrive early for lunch or book ahead for a window seat, and don't miss the evocative portrait of 'Chloe'.

$ Café All Angolo, corner of Hardware Lane and Little Bourke St, T9670 1411. Ideal for a fast and reliable bowl of pasta in simple and unpretentious surrounds, very popular with nearby office workers. Good value breakfasts.

$ Clarendon Fish and Chippers, 293 Clarendon St. Daily by 1130, until at least 2100. Healthy fast food, one of the very best in Melbourne, with fresh fish and great chips. A bit south of the centre.

$ Laurent, 306 Little Collins St, T9654 1011. Mon-Fri 0700-1900, Sat 0800-1800, Sun 0900-1700. An elegant Parisian-style patisserie that is begging for haute couture, but instead serves baguettes, coffee and exquisite pastries. Licensed.

$ Movida Tapas Bar, 1 Hosier Lane. T9663 3038. Daily 1200-late. Considered by many as the best tapas venue in the city. Authentic and happening atmosphere.

$ Nudel Bar, 76 Bourke St, T9662 9100. Small and spartan, serving excellent noodle dishes and some pasta. Good vegetarian selection.

$ Pellegrinis, 66 Bourke St, T9662 1885. Mon-Sat 0800-2330, Sun 1200-2000. Melbourne's original Italian café – it opened in 1954 and hasn't really changed much since then. It still remains a vibrant, crowded small space serving wonderful coffee and cheap pasta dishes.

$ Spencer, 475 Spencer St, T9329 5111, www.hotelspencer.com.au. Food served Mon-Fri 1200-1500 and 1830-2100 (Sat 1830-2100). Victorian pub, now with a seriously smart, highly regarded and usually lively restaurant in the lounge area. The quality rubs off on the cheap counter meals, which are well worth the stroll from the city.

North of the centre *p33, map p32*
Carlton's Lygon St is sometimes called 'Little Italy' for its string of Italian restaurants. Brunswick St in Fitzroy is probably the most diverse eating street in Melbourne.

$$ Abla's, 109 Elgin St, Carlton, T9347 0006. Thu-Fri 1200-1500, Mon-Wed and Sat 1800-2300. This small olive-green formal dining room consistently serves the best Lebanese food in town, with multi-course banquets.

$$ Cutler and Co, 55 Gertrude St, Fitzroy, T9419 4888, www. cutlerandco.com.au.

Dinner Tue-Sun from 1800; lunch Fri/Sat from 1200; bar Tue-Sun 1600-midnight.

$$ Gluttony It's a Sin, 278 Smith St, Collingwood, T9416 0336. Tue-Sat 0830-2300, Sun 1000-2100. Rich food in a café atmosphere. Everything is oversized and over-indulgent, but exceptional quality is always maintained.

$$ Shakahari, 201 Faraday St, Carlton, T9347 3848. Long-standing vegetarian restaurant with a warm, earthy but stylish interior. The limited but very fine menu will not disappoint. Multi award-winning restaurant/bar owned by celebrity chef Andrew McConnell. His former restaurant Three, One, Two in Carlton was his prelude to Cutler and Co and his success continues unabated. Set in a former metal work factory, the architecture successfully marries both the old and new creating a chic atmosphere that is both informal and relaxed. The brilliantly imaginative and inventive cuisine offers one of Australia's best dining experiences, provided you can get a booking!

$ Babka, 358 Brunswick St, Fitzroy, T9416 0091. Tue-Sun 0700-1900. Closed most of Jan. Friendly, unassuming and unpretentious bakery is perfection in everything it does.

$ Guru da Dhaba, 240 Johnston St, Fitzroy, T9486 9155. Very cheap but filling northern Indian dishes in a warm and noisy dining room with terracotta walls and simple black tables. BYO.

$ Kazen, 201 Brunswick St, T9417 3270. Tue-Sun 1200-1500, 1800-2230 (Sun 1800-2300 only). Small, Italian-influenced Japanese with dark, bluestone walls but a much lighter atmosphere. Excellent and interesting food, licensed but cheap corkage for BYO.

$ Mario's Café, 303 Brunswick St, Fitzroy, T9417 3343. Daily 0700-2400. Locally popular with a cosmopolitan clientele. Also good all-day breakfast and veggie options, licensed.

$ Moroccan Soup Bar, 183 St George's Rd, North Fitzroy, T9482 4240. Huge and superbly authentic Moroccan, with vegetarian meals.

$ Notturno, 179 Lygon St, T9347 8286. Daily 0600-0200. Of the many Italian cafés and restaurants in Lygon St, this large establishment is one of the least expensive. Good breakfasts, pasta, pizzas, cakes and coffee.

$ Thresherman's Bakehouse, 221 Faraday St, Carlton, T9349 2319. Daily 0630-2400. Spacious, relaxed café in an old car-repair shop. Great juices, soups and cafeteria meals as well as cakes and sandwiches.

$ Veggie Bar, 380 Brunswick St, T9417 6935. Daily 1100-2200, www.vegiebar.com.au. A relaxed, friendly vegetarian café-bar in a large old bare-brick warehouse. Great menu includes wood-fired pizzas, wraps, burgers and salads.

$ Viet Rose, 363 Brunswick St, T9417 7415. Generous quantities of laksa, vegetarian rolls and rice will defeat your stomach before your wallet.

Southeast of the centre *p33*

Richmond is one of the most international of the foodie suburbs. Most eateries are on Bridge Rd, but just to the north is Melbourne's 'Little Saigon', Victoria St, where there are around 50 Vietnamese restaurants. Greek food can be found on Swan St. In Prahran and Toorak there is no particular foodie area, the cafés and restaurants are dotted amongst the shops on Chapel St and Toorak Rd, but the choice is phenomenal. The eating in St Kilda has been traditionally clustered along Acland St and Fitzroy St, but since the ongoing renovation of St Kilda Baths, the choice on the foreshore has tripled. Italian predominates.

$$$-$$ Richmond Hill Café and Larder, 48 Bridge Rd, East Melbourne, T9421 2808, thecafe@rhcl.com.au. Daily 0830-1700. Hugely indulgent café and restaurant with wonderful cheese shop attached. Lunch includes the cheese platter and dinners are a culinary event.

$$ Borsch, Vodka & Tears, 173 Chapel St, Prahran, T9530 2694. Daily 1000-2130. Vibrant, friendly eastern European restaurant specializing in Polish broth and vodka … and tears (of laughter!). Live, gypsy-style music Mon, Wed and Sun. Evening bookings essential on music nights and weekends.

$$ Flavours of India, 68 Commercial Rd, Prahran, T9529 7811. Small, smart curry bar, popular with locals for food of exceptional quality. Also takeaway.

$$ Kanzaman, 458 Bridge Rd, Richmond, T9429 3402. Daily 1200-1500, 1800-2400. Excellent Lebanese with an exotic, richly decorated interior.

$$ Mexicali Rose, 103 Swan St, Richmond, T9429 5550, www.mexicalirose.com.au. Fri 1130-1430, daily 1800-2100. Friendly, earthy Mexican with generous servings of all the classics, plus a few interesting variations.

$$ Minh Tan 2, 192 Victoria St, Richmond, T9427 7131. Daily 1000-2230. One of the busiest and most respected Vietnamese restaurants, with a huge menu including fantastic mud crabs.

$$ Stokehouse, 30 Jacka Blvd, St Kilda, T9525 5555. Bar Mon-Fri 1200-2200, Sat 1100-2400, Sun 1000-2200; dining room daily 1200-1500, 1900-2200. With the best spot on the foreshore this award-winning bar-bistro is packed out year round. Simple ground-floor bar and beach-facing terrace. No bookings so arrive early for a good spot. Upstairs is an expensive, airy formal dining room, focusing on modern Australian seafood, which has the best balcony tables in Melbourne (bookings taken).

$ E Lounge, 409 Victoria St, Richmond, T9429 6060, elounge@tpg.com.au. Not an internet café, but some of the best thin and crispy wood-fired pizzas in the city. Very friendly, very orange. Also takeaway.

$ Greasy Joe's, 68 Acland St, St Kilda, T9525 3755. Daily 0700-2400. American retro bar and grill with excellent burgers, breakfasts and lots of pavement tables.

$ Il Fornaio, 2 Acland St, St Kilda, T9534 2922. 0700-2200. Small but warehousey, with lots of cheap eats and pavement tables, great for breakfast. French/Italian bakery.

$ Montalto, 33 Shoreham Rd, Red Hill, T5989 8412, www.montalto.com.au. One of many vineyard restaurants, Montalto is definitely one of the best, offering award-winning à la carte and a café alongside the cellar door. Outdoor and fine views add to the experience. Recommended.

$ Pier Pavilion, perched right at the end of St Kilda pier, St Kilda. 1000-sunset, 1000-2300 peak summer. Great spot for breakfast or simply one of the excellent coffees with a substantial slice of cake. Also cheap lunches.

$ Salona, 260 Swan St, Richmond, T9429 1460. Mon-Fri 1100-2200, Sat-Sun till 2300. The best of a small cluster of traditional Greek restaurants.

$ Topolinos, 87 Fitzroy, St Kilda, T9534 4856. Well-established and always busy. Recommended for good value pizza and pasta.

$ Torch, 178 Swan St, Richmond, T9428 7378. Daily 0830-1800. Small and welcoming, this is one of a few excellent cafés on this street. Busy but relaxed with cheap light lunches and all-day breakfasts. Good value.

Mornington Peninsula *p35*

$$ The Baths, on Sorrento foreshore overlooking a long skinny jetty, T5984 1500. Daily 0800-2100. For expensive but relaxed dining. Also a fish 'n' chip kiosk.

$$ Continental, 1-21 Ocean Beach Rd, Sorrento, T5984 2201. A funky choice. Meals, including breakfast, are served in a large room hung with modern art. A nightclub operates upstairs on Sat.

$ Coppins Café, 250 Ocean Beach Rd, T5984 5551, Daily 1000-1630. Sits above Sorrento Back Beach and is a wonderful place for a casual lunch or tea and scones on a sunny afternoon.

$ Heronswood Café, 105 Latrobe Parade, Dromana, T5984 7318. A little hard to find but well worth it, this little-known gem of a café is located in the historic Heronswood Gardens estate. Try the lamb. Recommended.

$ Just Fine Food, 23 Ocean Beach Rd, Sorrento, T5984 4666. Gourmet deli and café with busy pavement tables.

Phillip Island *p37*
$ Foreshore Bar Café, 11 Beach Rd, Rhyll, T5956 9520. Thu-Mon 1000-2000. Facing the sea, the locals' favourite spot for fish and chips. It also has a funky bar serving platters and nibbles.

$ Mad Cows, the Esplanade 4, Cowes, T5952 2560. Also facing the water and convenient for the beach. The locals' favourite for coffee and breakfast.

$ Island Food Store, 75 Chapel St, Cowes. For high-quality cake and coffee or a salad, set back from Chapel St past the supermarket.

$ Terrazzo, 5 Thompson Av, Cowes, T5952 3773. Wed-Sun 1700-2030. Good cheap place for Italian.

Dandenong Ranges *p38*
As you would expect there are dozens of restaurants, cafés and bistros on the mountain. A couple of the best are almost opposite each other on the main road through Olinda, which is a good place to pick up picnic ingredients. A visit to **Ripe**, at 376 Mount Dandenong Tourist Rd, Sassafras, is also a must for any visitor.

$$-$ Ranges, Olinda, T9751 2133. All day from 0900. Bright, large, cheerful and popular place for good value breakfasts, light lunches and, from Tue-Sat, mid-range Asian-influenced dinners.

$ Sky High Mount Dandenong, via Mount Dandenong Tourist Rd, T9751 0452. Daily. Bistro and café option at the Sky High complex. Memorable views. Open for breakfast, lunch or dinner.

$ View Point Tea Rooms, T9761 9902, opposite the Lookout at Kalorama, Five Ways intersection. Tue-Sun 0900. More wonderful views and divine breakfasts, baguettes, cakes and coffee.

Yarra Valley and around *p38*
$$ Yarra Valley Dairy, just south of Yarra Glen on McMeikans Rd, T9739 0023, www.yarravalleydairy.com.au. As an alternative to a winery lunch (see page 38) try this place. It is a licensed, fully working dairy with a lively and relaxed café and views over cow-filled fields. Mid-range platters and light lunches, book ahead at weekends. Cheese tastings daily 1030-1700, café closes a little before.

$$-$ Pasta Shop, next door to **Bodhi Tree**. Tue-Fri 0900-1730, Sat-Sun 0830-1700, restricted hours in winter. Cheery 2-room cottage café that does Healesville's best breakfast, tasty lunches and sells fresh handmade pasta and gourmet foods.

$ Bodhi Tree, 317 Maroondah Highway, Healesville, T5962 4407. Wed-Fri 1700-late, Sat-Sun 1200-late. Rustic, laid-back café with wholesome food and an assortment of tables in the large outdoor area, live acoustic music Fri nights.

🎧 Bars and clubs

The city is bursting with watering holes, from the sleekest cocktail bar to the grungiest of Victorian-era pubs with sticky carpets. The city centre bars tend to be the most sophisticated, with many wine bars and cocktail bars crossing the line into club territory and a sprinkling of traditional pubs frequented by office workers during the week. The large student population to the north of the city means that Carlton, Fitzroy and Collingwood have the heaviest concentration of live band venues and alternative pubs and bars. The inner suburbs south of the Yarra have some of the most fashionable bars and respected live music venues. Many pubs and bars also serve good food at reasonable prices, and liberal licensing laws mean it is possible to get a drink well into the small hours. Many club nights move regularly and the clubs themselves open and close frequently. Entry is usually about $12-15. King St has a lot of clubs but is known for being slightly seedy. Most of the clubs listed are city based but Chapel St in South Yarra is also a hot spot.

Free newspapers, mostly catering for the clubbing and music scenes, come and go but currently include *Beat* and *Inpress*. *Bnews* and *MCV* cover the gay and lesbian scene. All are widely available in cafés and music shops. There are general listings and entertainment guides in the Thu *Herald Sun* and Fri *Age* newspapers.

City centre *p25, map p26*
Bridie O'Reilly's, 62 Little Collins St. Out-of-the-way Irish theme bar with 20-odd beers on tap. Pub grub 1200-1430, 1800-2100 and mainly Irish acoustic live music Tue-Thu, cover bands Fri-Sat.
Hairy Canary, 212 Little Collins St. Mon-Fri 0730-0300, Sat 1000-0300, Sun 1000-0100. A smart, trendy bar and café, serving food all day. Rocks into the early hours.
Limerick Arms, 364 Clarendon St, South Melbourne. Cheap meals daily 1200-1430, 1800-2100. Had a revamp a few years ago to reflect its name and cash in on the rise of Irish theme bars. This isn't too forced, however, and the result is a pleasant, traditional Aussie drinking bar with an Irish flavour. DJs Fri-Sat.
Maori Chief, corner of Moray St and York St, South Bank, T9696 5363. Meals 1200-1400 Mon-Fri, 1800-2130 Mon-Sat. Combines a groovily shabby bar, dimly lit and furnished with retro couches, with good cheap casual food.
Mitre, 5 Bank Place. A traditional British-style pub, now hemmed in by the high-rises, which has been quietly pulling pints since the 1860s.
Section 8, 27-29 Tattersalls Lane, T0422-972 656. Undoubtedly one of the city's most unusual pubs. Utilizing former parking spaces down a nondescript city centre lane and made out of a single shipping container, it also has to be one of the simplest. Section 8 is often the first place Melbournians take visitors for a night out to show them the city's unique and often raw laneway culture. No yuppified decor here,

no comfy leather seats, just the basics, and it works remarkably well. Recommended.
Stork, 504 Elizabeth St, T9663 6237. Welcoming, relaxed front bar with pool table and open fire. Independent bands daily with a wide mix of styles. Seriously cheap, good quality bar food and cheap, surprisingly sophisticated bistro.

North of the centre *p33, map p32*
Bar Open, 317 Brunswick St, Carlton. Small, grungy bar with an open fire, armchairs and live music Wed-Sun.
Black Cat, 252 Brunswick St. Wed 1800-2300, Thu-Fri 1800-0100, Sat-Sun 1400-0100. Slick, seductive cabaret bar with live blues and jazz Thu-Sun.
Brandon, corner of Station St and Lee St, Carlton, T9347 2382. Goes out of its way to source real ales, both keg and bottled. Simple friendly front bar and large retro lounge. Equally simple pub grub, but with interesting touches.
Night Cat, 141 Johnston St, Fitzroy, T9417 0090. Lush, stylish bar with roomy couches and swing and salsa bands Thu-Sun.
North Fitzroy Star, 32 St George's Rd, Fitzroy, T9482 6484. Food daily 1100-2300. Contemporary, often exuberant styling in this traditional Victorian pub. Welcoming, with lots of nooks and crannies and open fires, the food is also well worth the trip. Cheap, inventive light lunches and bar nibbles and a mid-range set menu later on.
The Tote, 71 Johnston St, Fitzroy, www.thetotehotel.com. This isn't a gambling den, but is considered the most famous and influential of Melbourne's live music venues. For over 30 years the pub has hosted some of the best local talent, with many seasoned musos considering the place their second (or only) home. In 2010, due to new liquor licensing laws, the Tote's owner had no option but to close, but it would prove highly controversial and ultimately only temporary. The issue and the legislation drew such a

massive backlash from the public that street protests were arranged and it drew intense media coverage. As a result, new investment was found and the Tote lives on, now more popular than ever.

Southeast of the centre *p33*

Dizzy's Jazz Club, 381 Burnley St, Richmond. Hosts live jazz; check the playlist on www.dizzys.com.au

Elephant and Wheelbarrow, 169 Fitzroy St, St Kilda. London-style pub with over 20 beers on tap, mostly British or Irish. Live music Wed-Sun and a 'meet-the-Neighbours' session (really) on Mon. Cheap, feel-good meals, including breakfast, daily 1100-1430, 1700-2100.

The Esplanade, Esplanade, St Kilda. Something of a Melbourne institution for live music, cheap food and a raucous atmosphere.

Frost Bites, corner of Chapel St and Simmons St, Prahran, T9827 7401, www.frostbites.com.au. *The* bar to be seen at. The cool warehouse look is complemented by industrial quantities of slush cocktails waiting on tap. Very cheap café meals and live music Wed-Thu and Sun. Late licence most nights.

George, corner of Fitzroy St and Grey St, St Kilda. Slick wine bar, in sharp contrast to the lively and grungy **gpb** beneath. The latter serves cheap pub grub daily 1200-0100, and there's interesting live music Sat 1600-1900 and Sun 1800-2100.

Greyhound, 1 Brighton Rd, St Kilda, T9534 4189, www.ghhotel.com.au. Relaxed comfortable pub and a good live venue for everything from roots to rock and Sun night karaoke.

The Local, 184 Carlisle St, St Kilda East, T9537 2633. A pub that takes beer very seriously. If you are an aficionado looking for fine choice, quality and a Euro-style atmosphere this is the place. Live music is also a regular feature.

The Pint on Punt, 42 Punt St, St Kilda, T9510 4273, www.pintonpunt.com.au. One of

Melbourne's best drinking holes. A simple, warm country-Irish-style pub with open brick fires and bare wood floors. Accommodation upstairs (**$$-$**), see page 43.

Prince of Wales, 29 Fitzroy St, St Kilda. A magnet for all types from the divine to the desperate and consequently has an unpredictable energy. Lots of pool tables, cheap pots on Mon and a busy live venue next door.

Vineyard, 71 Acland St, St Kilda, T9534 1942. Daily 1000-0300. The seriously laid-back and cool frequent this joint. A long, casual space that can be opened onto the side street on a sunny day. Also great café food.

⊕ Entertainment

Melbourne *p24, maps p26 and p32*
For details of events, visit the VIC and pick up a free copy of the *Official Visitor's Guide*, a useful rundown of highlights, and *Melbourne Events*, an excellent monthly publication that has details of every event and attraction in the city. See also Bars and clubs above for live music venues in pubs and bars. The main agencies are **Ticketek**, T132849, www.premier.ticketek.com.au, and **Ticketmaster**, T136100, www.ticket master.com.au. There is an outlet at the Athenaeum Theatre, 188 Collins St, Mon-Fri 0900-1700, Sat 1000-1600. There is no telephone number – you have to go in person.

Cinema

Astor, 1 Chapel St, border of Prahran and St Kilda, T9510 1414. A different contemporary or classic movie every day, with lots of double bills.

George, 135 Fitzroy St, St Kilda, T9534 6922. Mainstream movies, cheap tickets for guests at some local hostels.

Village cinema, at the Jam Factory, 500 Chapel St, Prahran, T1300 555400, www.villagecinemas.com.au, and the Crown Complex, Southbank, T1300 555400.

Live music

Major acts play at the **Rod Laver Arena**, the **Melbourne Concert Hall**, the **Etihad Stadium** and the **MCG** and tickets for these events are usually sold through ticketing agencies. **Melbourne Concert Hall**, part of Victorian Arts Centre, is the home of the Melbourne Symphony Orchestra.

⚙ Festivals

Melbourne *p24, maps p26 and p32*
Melbourne puts on an extraordinary spread of festivals throughout the year. Many of these attract the best talent in the country and bring over prestigious international artists. To see what's on and how to buy tickets pick up a copy of the free monthly *Melbourne Events* from the VIC. For forward planning see www.thatsmelbourne.com.au. All of the festivals listed below are annual.

Sports fans should also watch out for the **Australian Open** in **Jan**, **F1 Grand Prix** in **Mar**, the **Australian Football League Grand Final** in **Sep** and the **Spring carnival** (Melbourne Cup) in **Nov**.

Jan Midsumma, T9415 9819, www.midsumma.org.au, is a gay and lesbian celebration of pride, presence and profile. Running for 3 weeks it involves street parties, events and the Midsumma Carnival.

Mar Melbourne Food and Wine Festival, T9823 6100, is a prestigious gastronomic celebration that showcases talent and the produce of the city and region. Events include master classes, food writers' forum, tasting tours and the 'world's longest lunch'. It's held over Labour Day weekend.

Moomba River Festival is an annual event that is over 50 years old and celebrates the city as a whole. The name derives from the aboriginal word meaning 'to get together and have fun'. Held alongside the Yarra in Alexandra Gardens, Birrarung Marr and the Waterfront City Piazza at Docklands, it includes live music, dance, a waterskiing competition, fireworks displays, the Moomba Parade along Swanston St and the wacky Birdman Rally.

Apr Melbourne International Comedy Festival, T9417 7711, www.comedyfestival.com.au, held over 3 weeks, is one of the world's largest laugh-fests. A month of comedy in every guise, from more than 1000 Australian and international performers.

Jul Melbourne International Film Festival, www.melbournefilmfestival.com.au, showcases about 350 of the best films from Australia and around the world. The 2-week festival includes features, documentaries, shorts and discussion sessions with film makers in 4 main theatre venues.

Sep-Oct Melbourne Fringe Festival, T9660 9600, www.melbournefringe.com.au, lasts for 10 days. It is an off-shoot of the main Melbourne Festival with a more anarchic spirit. Showcases new and innovative art in all fields and has lots of free events, parties and a legendary parade down Brunswick St, in Fitzroy.

Melbourne Festival, T9662 4242, www.melbournefestival.com.au, takes place over 3 weeks. It is the city's major arts festival showing the cream of local and overseas talent in theatre, dance, opera, music and the visual arts in indoor and outdoor venues all over Melbourne.

Oct-Nov Spring Racing Carnival, www.racingvictoria.net.au, is the horse-racing festival linked to several major races and race days. The highlight is 'the race the nation stops for', the Melbourne Cup (a public holiday in Melbourne), held at Flemington Racecourse. Traditionally celebrated with champagne, fancy frocks, oversized hats and a bet, it is run on the first Tue in Nov. Entry tickets cost about $60 from **Ticketmaster**, www.ticketmaster.com.au, and must be bought in advance.

O Shopping

Melbourne p24, maps p26 and p32
Art and crafts

There are some fine Aboriginal art galleries at the eastern end of Flinders Lane. There are a couple of upmarket shops on Bourke St, such as **Aboriginal Art**, at No 90, but there are also other options. **Koorie Heritage Trust** (see page 29) is one. Another is the **Aboriginal Handicrafts Shop**, the mezzanine part of the Uniting Church Shop at 130 Little Collins St, T9650 3277. It may be small, but they have an excellent range of affordable pieces, from bark and paper art to didgeridoos, carved wood and woven baskets. All profits go directly back to the originating communities. Open Mon-Fri 1000-1630.

Bookshops

Booktalk, 91 Swan St, Richmond. Mon-Sat 0830-1730, Sun 0900-1600. Also a café with good value breakfasts.

Brunswick Street Bookstore, 305 Brunswick, Fitzroy, T9416 1030. Daily 1000-2300. Large independent with a well-chosen range.

Dymocks, 234 Collins St, City. One of the largest chain stores with an excellent range, including music CDs, and knowledgeable staff. Open late on Fri.

Grub Street, 379 Brunswick St, Fitzroy. Great collection, covering a wide range of contemporary issues, non-fiction and fiction.

Readings, 701 Glenferrie Rd, Hawthorn, T9819 1917. Very popular and one of several outlets in the city. Café attached.

Information Victoria, 505 Little Collins St, T1300 366 356, www.vic.gov.au. Mon-Fri. Stocks an excellent range of maps and guides and offers good general advice. Mail order available.

Clothes

Melbourne is famous for its wonderful clothes shopping. People fly from all over Australia just to have a shopping weekend in Melbourne. **Crown Entertainment Complex** has some of the city's most exclusive boutiques, such as Armani and Versace. Equally swanky shopping can be found on **Collins St**, **Toorak Rd** and the city end of **Chapel St**, which is lined with designer label shops and chain stores, becoming steadily cheaper as you head south. In the city centre the eastern end of Collins St has expensive designer boutiques. More funky independent designers populate Little Collins St and Flinders Lane, such as the fascinating and colourful **Christine**, 181 Flinders Lane, and **Alice Euphemia**, Shop 6, 37 Swanston St, supporting Australasian design talent.

Brunswick St, Fitzroy, is still a good spot for finding choice second-hand articles, and it gets positively bargain basement over in neighbouring **Smith St**. South of Commercial Rd on Chapel St, Prahran, and on the side road Greville St, are a couple of dozen small and chic shops, including the wildly exuberant **Shag**, 130 Chapel St, daily 1200-1800, which is difficult to leave without having been tempted into buying something that'll turn heads. There are a couple of interesting shops on **Barkly St**, St Kilda, near the junction with Acland St, and on **Acland St** by the junction with Albert St.

Markets

Gleadell St Market, Richmond. Sat 0700-1300. A cheap, old-fashioned street market where few stallholders speak much English. Fruit, veggies, bread, flowers and fish.

Prahran Market, Commercial Rd. Dawn-1700 Tue, Sat, dawn-1800 Thu-Fri. Fabulous and fancy fresh-food market.

Queen Victoria Market 513 Elizabeth St. Tue, Thu 0600-1400, Fri 0600-1800, Sat 0600-1500, Sun 0900-1600. The market has expanded and evolved since the 1870s and now consists of a substantial brick building housing the meat and dairy sections and a vast area of open-air sheds, selling fruit and vegetables, clothing and souvenirs. The meat hall has fresh meat, fish and seafood and the dairy hall includes nearly 40 deli stalls selling bread, cheese, sliced meats, pickles, dips and sauces. The sheds can be a good place to find cheap leather goods but generally hold a lot of low-quality, mass-market junk. The food sections, however, are well worth a wander for the friendly banter of the stallholders and extremely tempting sights and smells. There is a food court and there are places in the dairy hall to grab a bite and sit down. There are also entertaining tours focusing on either history or tastes, such as the Foodies' Dream Tour, Tue, Thu-Sat 1000, $35 including samples along the way. Bookings essential, T9320 5822.

St Kilda Market takes place every Sun along the curve of the Esplanade. The stalls offer mostly craft and gifts with a few clothes stalls. **Victorian Arts Centre Market**, Southbank. High-quality art and craft stalls on Sun 1000-1800.

⚠ What to do

Melbourne *p24, maps p26 and p32*
Aerial tours
Melbourne Seaplanes, Williamstown's Gem Pier, T9547 4454, www.seaplane.com.au. Specializes in 4 main flights: a short 15-min loop around the city from $140, to a 55-min loop around Port Phillip Bay for $270, which, at an extra cost, can be broken by a stop in Sorrento for lunch. Minimum 2 people.

Ballooning
Despite its variable weather the city has a well-established reputation for early morning scenic flights.
Balloon over Melbourne, T9427 0088, www.balloonovermelbourne.com.au. Very experienced, departures from Richmond, including breakfast in the Observatory Café, Royal Botanical Gardens, from $330.

Go Wild, T9739 0772, www.gowild ballooning.com.au. Champagne breakfast flights of 1 hr from $350. Recommended.

Body and soul
Aurora Spa Retreat, part of **The Prince** boutique hotel (page 43), 2 Acland St, St Kilda, T9536 1130, www.auroraspa retreat.com. One of the country's largest and most decadent spa and treatment centres.

City tours
As you'd expect there are a wealth of city tour options from tours by bike to those for chocoholics. The visitor information centre has full listings and can book on your behalf.

Cricket
The annual highlight is the **Melbourne Boxing Day Test Match**. International test matches are played regularly in summer at the MCG, T136122, www.mcg.org.au. Tickets from **Ticketmaster**, www.ticketmaster.com.au.

Cycling
A great way to see some of the sights and parks of the city and inner suburbs is to cycle around them. **Real Melbourne Cycle Tours**, T417339203, biketours@internex.net.au or www.rentabike.net.au, provide the bike, refreshments and a guide for a variety of tours. Price around $99 for a half-day. They also offer independent hire from $15 ($35 day). Other outlets include **Borsari Cycles**, 193 Lygon St, Carlton, T9347 4100, **Freedom Machine**, 265 Bay St, Port Melbourne, T9681 8533, and **St Kilda Cycles**, 11 Carlisle St, T9534 3074.

Horse racing
The Spring Carnival's **Melbourne Cup** is one of the country's major events, held on the first Tue in Nov at Flemington Racecourse. Grandstand tickets aren't cheap but ground entry is more reasonable (from $60). Tickets from **Ticketmaster**. For more information T1800 352229, www.racingvictoria.net.au.

Motor racing

The first Grand Prix of the F1 season is held at Albert Park in early Mar. Tickets cost about $100 for day entry, $160 for 4-day entry and from $350 for a 4-day reserved grandstand ticket. Note the Grand Prix is very much geared around the corporates so public access and views are limited. If you do not have a corporate ticket be prepared to be disappointed in what you see and where you can go. That said, in recent years entry has includes a post-race concert by a high-profile band such as Kiss and Simple Minds. See www.grandprix.com.au for more details. Tickets from **Ticketmaster.**

Penguin spotting

Penguin Waters, T9386 8488, www.penguinwaters.com.au. Sunset fairy penguin-watching tours departing from Southgate (2 hrs, $55). Barbecue and refreshments included.

Tour operators

Autopia Tours, T1800 000507, www.autopiatours.com.au. Day trips to Phillip Island, Great Ocean Rd and the Grampians (all around $125), plus 3-day trip options.
Go West, T1300 736551, www.gowest.com.au. This is one of the best day tours along the Great Ocean Rd. It picks up from about a dozen Melbourne back-packer hostels between 0715 and 0820 every day, returning about 2130. Tours cost around $125.
Wildlife Tours, T9741 6333, www.wildlifetours.com.au. This has similar options with a day tour of the Great Ocean Rd from $95, plus a trip to Ballarat, and another to the Dandenongs. Both companies offer a 2-day tour of the Great Ocean Rd plus the Grampians for around $169, and have backpacker bus routes to Adelaide and Sydney. Larger coach companies (with larger coaches and slightly higher fares) such as **APT**, T1300 336932,

www.aptours.com.au, **AAT Kings**, T1300 556100, www.aatkings.com.au, and **Gray Line**, T1300 858687, www.grayline.com, offer a wider range of day tours as far as Ballarat, Echuca, Mount Buller and the Yarra Valley.

Walking

For details of Melbourne's excellent free guided walks courtesy of the Greeter Service, see page 25. The VIC has free brochures and maps for a variety of self-guided walks, such as art walks along Swanston St and the Yarra River and heritage walks.

The Golden Mile walk is a 4-km route through the city, which goes past the most significant architectural and historical features. It can be done as a self-guided walk ($4) or guided ($20, 2 hrs) on Wed and Fri-Sat at 1030 and 1330. Bookings essential, T1300 780045.

Mornington Peninsula *p35*
Diving

The diving is superb, with shipwrecks and j-class submarines, sheer-wall and fast-drift dives, leafy sea dragons and stingrays. Operators include:
Bayplay Adventure Lodge, 46 Canterbury Jetty Rd, Blairgowrie, T5988 0188, www.bayplay.com.au.
Dive Victoria, 3752 Point Nepean Rd, Portsea, T5984 3155, www.divevictoria.com.au.

Dolphin tours

Bottlenose dolphins live in Port Phillip Bay and swimming with them is becoming increasingly popular, from Oct-Apr.
Moonraker, T5984 4211, www.moonrakercharters.com.au. Offers day tours from Melbourne with dolphin watch or swim options (ex Sorrento) from $199. From Sorrento expect to pay around $100.

Horse trekking
Gunnamatta Trail Rides, T5988 6755, www.gunnamatta.com.au. Offers treks and gallops along the ocean beaches from 30 mins for $35 to full day from $190. Beginners welcome.

Hot pools and day spa
Peninsula Hot Springs, Springs Lane, T5950 8777, www.peninsulahotsprings.com, from $30. Daily 0730-2200. A range of indoor and outdoor pools, a day spa and a café. Recommended.

Surfing
Mornington Peninsula Surf School, T9787 6494, www.greenroomsurf.com.au. Offers surfing lessons.

Phillip Island *p37*
Seal spotting
The only way to get close to the seals is to take one of a range of excellent boat trips with **Wildlife Coast Cruises**, T5952 5583, www.wildlifecoastcruises.com.au, which operates out of Cowes ($67, 2 hrs). It also runs cruises out to French Island, Wilson's Promontory (see page 60), and operates whale-watching trips in winter.

Surfing
Out There, T5956 6450, or Island, T5952 2578. Would-be surfers can take a lesson with one of these outfits. Island also has 3 shops around the island and hires out equipment and wetsuits.

Tour operators
Afternoon or evening tours from Melbourne are offered by all the major operators. One of the best is **Autopia**, T9326 5536, www.autopiatours.com.au.

Yarra Valley and around *p38*
Several companies run day trips from Melbourne. **Tasting Tours Backpacker**

Winery Tours, T9419 4444, www.backpacker winerytours.com.au, takes medium-sized groups out to 4 wineries including Domaine Chandon. From $100, including lunch, wine and afternoon tea. Pick-ups from Melbourne (Flinders St Station, Queensbury Hill and St Kilda).

If you fancy seeing the wineries from a hot-air balloon rather than the bottom of a wine glass, check out **Global**, T1800 627661, or **Go Wild**, T9890 0339, www.gowildballooning. com.au. From $330.

⊖ Transport

Melbourne *p24, maps p26 and p32*
Most of the major sights can be reached on foot and using the free City Circle tram, which travels along Flinders St, up Springs St, along La Trobe St and around Telstra Dome down Harbour Esplanade.

Air
Flight information is available at www.melair.com.au or by ringing the relevant airline. See also page 24. **Qantas Virgin Blue Tiger Airways** and **Jetstar** are the principal suppliers of interstate flights with direct daily services to all state capitals. It's all very competitive so shop around on the net.

Bus
Local There is a bus for almost anywhere you could wish to go within Greater Melbourne, but the further out they travel the less frequently they go. City Saver, 2-hr and daily tickets can be bought on board and notes are accepted.
Long distance **Greyhound** has a service to **Sydney** and V-Line has a daily bus/train service to **Canberra** from Spencer St Station and also operates most state services to Victorian country towns, with a few Gippsland services from Flinders St Station.
Backpacker Autopia, T1800 000507, www.autopiatours.com.au, runs trips to **Sydney** (3½ days, from $445, including backpacker accommodation).

Car

The city has 3 arterial CityLink road tollways, www.citylink.com.au, which electronically read 'e-tags' in vehicles: great for residents, but a real pain for visitors. The road signs are marked in blue with orange text. Passes can be purchased in advance or until midnight the day after you travel (the fine for travelling without a pass is about $100), from the website, post offices and the CityLink Customer Centre, 67 Lorimer St, just off the Westgate Freeway. Buy passes (single use up to $4, 24 hr or weekend $11.30) over the phone with a credit card, 0800-2000, T132629, or via the website. Motorcyclists can use the CityLinks for free. To avoid the tolls when entering the city from the Westgate Freeway (Geelong, Highway 1) take the Kings Way exit for Richmond, Prahran and St Kilda, and the Power St exit for the city, Carlton and Fitzroy. From the South Eastern Freeway (the east, Highway 1) take the Toorak Rd exit and turn left for the city centre and suburbs. From the Calder/ Tullamarine Freeways (the northwest and the airport) take the first exit after the junction of the two freeways. This drops onto Bulla Rd, which eventually becomes Elizabeth St. Beware of metered parking in the city centre; it extends as late as 2400. If you are heading south to the Mornington Peninsula the fastest route is via the new Eastlink Tollway. A trip costs $5.50 and can be purchased online at www.breeze.com.au. Beware, however: do not exceed 100 kph as the bridges are littered with number plate ID cameras that double as speed cameras.

Car hire A cheap option is **Rent-a-Bomb**, T131553, T9696 7555 (South Melbourne depot), www.rentabomb.com.au, which hires out cars for $175 per week for use within 50 km of the city centre.

Ferry

Spirit of Tasmania, T1800 634906, www.spiritoftasmania.com.au. Operates nightly overnight ferries from Port Melbourne to Devonport in Tasmania (13 hrs, prices vary according to season and start at $99 per passenger and at $69 per car).

Taxi

Arrow, T132211; **Silver Top**, T131008; **Yellow 13 Cabs**, T132227.

Train

Local Used mostly to service the outer suburbs. Various networks extend regular services to destinations including **Belgrave** (the Dandenongs), **Frankston** (connections to the Mornington Peninsula), **Lilydale** (connections to the Yarra Valley and beyond), **Stony Point** (ferry connections to French and Phillip Islands), **Werribee** and **Williamstown**. Tickets must be bought at departure stations.

Tram

Trams are the main way to get about the city centre and inner suburbs. They operate more like a bus than a train so you'll need to hail one if you want to get on, and push the buzzer to indicate to the driver that you want to get off. The network of trams mostly radiates out from the city centre to the inner suburbs but some routes travel from suburb to suburb through the centre. **City Saver** and 2-hr tickets can be bought on board, but the dispensers take coins only. Daily tickets must be purchased in advance from a newsagent displaying the Metcard logo.

Mornington Peninsula *p35*
Bus

From **Frankston** station the **Portsea Passenger Bus Service**, T5986 5666, www.grenda.com.au, operates services (No 788) down the Port Phillip Bay coast, with stops including **Dromana**, **Sorrento** (stop 18, corner of Melbourne Rd and Ocean Beach Rd) and **Portsea** (stop 1, National Park entrance). Full run takes 1½ hrs. Mon-Fri services every 1-2 hrs, 0700-1900 (plus Fri 2040); every 2 hrs from 0800-2000 weekends. Last buses back from Portsea at Mon-Fri 1915, Sat 1800 and Sun 1735.

Ferry
A car ferry operates from **Sorrento** to **Queenscliff** on the Bellarine Peninsula. Ferries from 0700-1700, 50 mins, passenger $9, children and concessions $8, cars under 5.5 m $59 plus passengers $7 each, T5258 3244, www.searoad.com.au.

Dandenong Ranges *p38*
Bus/train
There are metropolitan train services daily between **Melbourne** City Circle stations, **Upper Fern Tree Gully** (1 hr) and **Belgrave**, running every 20-30 mins. **US Bus Lines**, T9754 1444, www.usbus.com.au, runs services between **Belgrave** station and **Olinda** (No 694), stopping at **Sherbrook** and **Sassafras**. Services at 0620, 0700 and 5 mins past the hour from Mon-Fri 1000-1500, and every 1-2 hrs Sat 0820-1620. They also have a service between **Upper Fern Tree Gully** and Olinda (No 698), following the commuter hours of 0730 and 0830, and 1610-1940 Mon-Fri only. Metropolitan fares apply, so get a day ticket in Melbourne. There are no local bus services on Sun.

Yarra Valley and around *p38*
There are metropolitan train services daily between **Melbourne** City Circle stations and **Lilydale** (40 mins), running every 20-30 mins. **McKenzie**, T5962 5088, www.mckenzies. com.au, runs less frequent daily bus services between **Lilydale**, **Yarra Glen**, **Healesville** and **Marysville**. Call for times.

ℹ Directory

Melbourne *p24, maps p26 and p32*
Medical services   Health centres:
Travellers Medical and Vaccination Centre, Royal Melbourne Hospital, Royal Pde, T9347 7022. **City Health Care**, 255 Bourke St, T9650 1711. Mon-Fri 0900-1800, Sat 1000-1700, and **Acland St Medical Centre**, 171 Acland St, St Kilda, T9534 0635. Mon-Thu 0900-1900, Fri 0900-1800, Sat 0900-1200, are both visitor-friendly and bulk bill. Medicare at **Centre Point Mall**, corner of Bourke St and Swanston St, Mon-Fri 0900-1645. **Hospitals   Royal Melbourne**, Grattan St, Parkville, T9342 7000; **St Vincent's**, 41 Victoria Pde, Fitzroy, T9288 2211. **Pharmacies   Mulqueeny**, corner Swanston St and Collins St, T9654 8569, Mon-Fri 0800-2000, Sat 0900-1800, Sun 1100-1800. **Sally Lew**, 41 Fitzroy St, St Kilda, T9534 8084, daily 0900-2100. Cheap film processing. **Police**   637 Flinders St, T9247 5347.

Southeast Victoria

Lying east of Melbourne and extending from the mountains to the coast, Gippsland is the rural heartland of Victoria, a rich landscape of rolling green dairy pasture. In the far south is the main attraction, Wilson's Promontory, a low range of forest-covered granite mountains, edged with isolated sandy bays and golden river inlets and marked only by the occasional walking track. Carefully maintained as a wilderness, the 'Prom' offers intimate encounters with wildlife and is a stunning place to walk, swim, camp or simply laze about. In the centre of the region, the Gippsland Lakes system forms the largest inland waterway in Australia, where every small town has jetties festooned with yachts and fishing boats. Heading inland, the landscape rises to the limestone caves of Buchan and the rugged forest and gorges of the Snowy River National Park. Further east along the coast, is Croajingolong National Park, a wilderness of dense bush and river inlets, the largest of which is overlooked by one of Victoria's loveliest small towns, Mallacoota, an isolated and peaceful haven.

Getting there and around

Getting around

The main V-Line train line heads out from Melbourne through Dandenong and Warragul to Bairnsdale about three times daily. From here buses take over. The route heads east via Lakes Entrance, Orbost, Cann River and Genoa to the NSW border. From Dandenong there are connecting bus services to Bass then Newhaven and Cowes on Phillip Island; to Wonthaggi and Inverloch; and to Yarram via Leongatha, Fish Creek and Foster. There are also ferries to Cowes from Stony Point on the Mornington Peninsula. From Cann River there is a set-down-only service to Canberra and another up the coast to Batemans Bay.
➠ *See Transport, page 67.*

➠ *See Transport, page 67.*

Tourist information

If heading east out of Melbourne along the Princes Highway you can stock up on information from the main Melbourne VIC. Within the region itself the main accredited VICs are to the east in Sale, the **Central Gippsland Information Centre** ① *8 Forster St, T1800 677520, www.gippslandinfo.com.au*, or, if travelling south out of Melbourne towards Wilson's Promontory along the South Gippsland Highway, the **Prom Country**

Information Centre ① *on the highway in Korumbarra, T5655 2233, infocentre@sgsc. vic.gov.au, 0900-1700*. The tourism website is www.inspiredbygippsland.com.au. Another option is **Bairnsdale and Lakes Entrance Information Centre** ① *240 Main St Bairnsdale and corner Princes Highway and Marine Pde, Lakes Entrance T1800 637060, www.discovereastgippsland.com.au.*

Wilson's Promontory National Park → *For listings, see pages 64-67.*

The 'Prom', as it is known by Victorians, is one of the state's top attractions, with granite-capped mountains covered in forest sloping down to the purest of white sand beaches and tannin-stained rivers meandering down to the sea. The northeastern region is a wilderness area only accessible to bushwalkers and boats. The park's most accessible beaches and bushwalks are on the western coast near Tidal River, the only 'settlement', where parrots, wombats and kangaroos roam (and fly) around freely. The year 2005 saw two notable events on the Prom, first in summer when wildfires decimated the region, and then, ironically, the first snowfalls for years in August.

Arriving in Wilson's Promontory National Park

There are two main routes down to the Prom. The more direct route heads through the heart of dairy country, taking in Koonwarra and Fish Creek. The longer route heads south to the coast via the 'Big Worm' and Wonthaggi. Tiny **Koonwarra**, 140 km from Melbourne and 80 km from Wilson's Promontory, is a worthy distraction thanks to the **Koonwarra Store** ① *daily 0800-1700*, a café/restaurant serving country breakfasts, lunches and dinners of the highest quality, and a takeaway. **Fish Creek** is another tiny and charming settlement. **Foster**, 30 km from Koonwara, is the closest major town to Wilson's Promontory and is well supplied with supermarkets and bakeries to fuel camping expeditions.

Visit the **Parks Office** ① *Tidal River, T5680 9555, www.parkweb.vic.gov.au, 0900-1700*, for permits, detailed notes on day and overnight walks and advice on activities in the park. Park entry at the gate is $9.50 per car per day.

Around the park

The park offers dozens of trail options. **Squeaky Beach**, **Picnic Bay** and **Whisky Bay** can be reached by very short walks from car parks but the best walk is to all of these beaches from Tidal River along the coast (9 km return). The best views of the Prom are from the top of **Mount Oberon**. The walk up from Telegraph Saddle car park, 3.5 km from Tidal River, is wide and easy with a few rock-cut steps at the top (7 km, two hours return). Sunrise is the best time for photographs of Norman Bay below. A good spot for sunset is Whisky Bay. A very popular day walk from the same car park is the track to **Sealers' Cove** (9.5 km, 2½ hours one way) passing through thick rainforest to the eastern side of the Prom. The cove has a long arc of golden sand, tightly fringed by bush. There is a basic campsite at Sealers' Creek. The cove is beautiful but the walk has little variety and the return leg can feel like a bit of a slog. A more interesting day's walk is the **Oberon Bay** loop that also starts from Telegraph Saddle (19 km, six hours). There is also an extended walk (38 km, two to three days) to the lighthouse that sits on a great dome of granite on the southern tip of the promontory. The **Lighthouse Trek** can be done independently or from October to May with a ranger guide ($300-450, including accommodation and meals). At the lighthouse you can stay in cottages that are equipped with bunks, kitchen and bathroom. The cottages can be booked by the bed or exclusively for groups (**$$**).

Gippsland Lakes → *For listings, see pages 64-67.*

The break between central and eastern Gippsland is marked by a series of connected lakes, separated from the sea only by the long thin dune system of the eastern end of Ninety Mile Beach. This strip of sand, designated the Gippsland Lakes Coastal Park, is accessible only by boat and is relatively unspoiled, even in peak season. The main service town in the area is Bairnsdale, but there are some pretty settlements dotted around the margins of the lakes, and Metung is particularly picturesque. Soon after Yarram is the turning to Woodside Beach, which marks the start of Ninety Mile Beach, the long golden stretch of sand that curves all the way to Lakes Entrance.

Sale, the administration centre for Gippsland, has all the usual services available but offers few attractions for visitors. The **VIC** ① *Princes Highway, T5144 1108, www.gippslandinfo.com.au, 0900-1700,* is just west of the town centre. **Bairnsdale** is the largest town in the Lakes area, though it isn't actually on a lake shore itself. It is worth stopping here for the Aboriginal **Krowathunkalong Keeping Place** ① *Dalmahoy St, T5152 1891, Mon-Fri 0900-1200 and 1300-1700, $3.50, children $2.50, concessions $1.50,* which features chillingly frank descriptions of the brutal Gunnai massacres that took place in Gippsland during the 1830s-1850s. The excellent **VIC** ① *240 Main St, T5152 3444, www.discovereastgippsland.com.au, 0900-1700,* will help with information and bookings for the whole Lakes region as well as Bairnsdale.

Paynesville hugs a stretch of lake shore facing **Raymond Island**, a small haven for wildlife, especially koalas, with one of the country's most concentrated wild populations. It's not a park, however, and the Paynesville township effectively extends across the car ferry (every half an hour, $8.50 return, pedestrians free) to claim a portion of the island as a suburb. Further offshore, **Rotamah Island** is home to a **Bird Observatory** ① *T131963, rotamah@i-o.net.au.* Camping is possible; contact the observatory.

Metung is on a small spit only a few hundred metres wide, giving it the feel of a village surrounded by water. Most of the homes spreading up the low wooded hill to the rear overlook Bancroft Bay, lined with yachts and jetties. Well-heeled visitors are catered for here, with a couple of good restaurants, wonderful day and sailing options and some luxurious accommodation options.

Standing at the only break in the long stretch of dunes that separate the Gippsland Lakes from the sea is **Lakes Entrance**. Once a small fishing village, it has become a traditional Victorian coastal holiday resort, known for its pleasant and varied scenery, range of accommodation, eateries and water-based activities.

Over the footbridge is the **Entrance Walking Track**, a leisurely and rewarding two-hour return stroll through dunes and bush to **Ninety Mile Beach** and **Flagstaff Lookout**. Wyanga Park Winery, see page 66, runs popular day and evening cruises from the town's Club Jetty on their launch, the *Corque*. The **VIC** ① *corner Marine Pde and the Esplanade, T5155 1966, discovereastgippsland.com.au, 0900-1700.*

East to Mallacoota → *For listings, see pages 64-67.*

Orbost

The Yalmy Road continues down to Orbost, sitting at the point at which the Snowy River meets the Princes Highway. Though well placed to capitalize on the considerable tourist traffic, the small town offers little to the traveller except the cheapest petrol and last decent supermarkets until well into NSW, and a helpful **VIC** ① *The Slab Hut, Nicholson St, T5154 2424, orbostvic@bigpond.com, 0900-1700.*

Marlo and Cape Conran

The tiny fishing community of Marlo at the mouth of the Snowy River is a popular long-weekend destination for Victorians, with a variety of caravan and cabin accommodation but few facilities aside from a couple of small grocery shops, one doing takeaways, and an impressive pub with guesthouse facilities. There are several good marked walking trails around Cape Conran, where two beautiful sandy beaches are generally fine for swimming. Camping is available; see **Parks Victoria**, page 65.

Croajingolong National Park

This wonderful park, a narrow strip south of the Princes Highway that runs for 100 km west of the state border, is best known for its long stretch of wild coastline, but it also encompasses eucalyptus forests, rainforests, granite peaks, estuaries and heathland. The remoteness of much of the park has led to a wide diversity of flora and fauna, with over 1000 native plants and more than 300 bird species, and it has been recognized as a World Biosphere Reserve.

Point Hicks was the first land in Australia to be sighted by the crew of Captain's Cook's *Endeavour* in 1770 and mainland Australia's tallest lighthouse was built here in 1890. The track to Point Hicks (2.25 km) starts at the end of the road past Thurra River campsite, and passes Honeymoon Bay. There are fantastic views from the top of the **lighthouse** ① *T5156 0432, www.pointhicks.com.au, tours 1300 Fri-Mon*, and southern right whales are often seen just off shore in winter. For details of staying in the lighthouse or campsite see page 65. It is possible to walk the coast from **Bemm River** right over the NSW border into the **Nadgee Nature Reserve**. Trekking on the wild beaches makes up the bulk of the experience, but walkers will also encounter a range of spectacular coastal scenery. There are a number of campsites with facilities along the route, though water can get scarce and walkers need to carry a couple of days' supply. Numbers are restricted on all stretches of the trek, and permits are required. Contact the Cann River or Mallacoota Park's Victoria office ① *T5161 9500, www.parkweb.vic.gov.au.*

Mallacoota

Perched on the edge of the Mallacoota Inlet and the sea, Mallacoota is a beguiling and peaceful place. Surrounded by the Croajingolong National Park and a long way from any large cities, it's a haven for wildlife, particularly birdlife. The quiet meandering waters of the inlet are surrounded by densely forested hills. To the south are several beautiful coastal beaches, like **Betka Beach**, a popular local swimming beach. Spectacular layered and folded rocks can be seen at **Bastion Point** and **Quarry Beach**. There are almost unlimited opportunities for coastal walks, bushwalking, fishing and boating. Once a year in April there is an explosion of creativity at the Carnival in Coota – a week-long festival of theatre, visual arts, music and literature.

The **Mallacoota Walking Track** is a 7-km loop, signposted from the main roundabout, which goes through casuarina forest and heathland, along the beach to Bastion Point and back towards town past the entrance. To explore the inlet by water there are several options. Motor boats, canoes and kayaks can be hired from the caravan near the wharf. Several cruising boats are also based at the wharf: visit their kiosks for bookings. For details, see What to do, page 66. There are magnificent views of the area from **Genoa Peak**; the access road is signposted from the Princes Highway, 2 km west of Genoa. From the picnic and parking area there is a 1.5-km walking track to the summit, steep for the last 100 m. Further afield is tiny **Gabo Island**, home to one of the largest fairy penguin colonies in the country, plus one of the highest lighthouses. For local information, contact the **VIC** ① *main Wharf, T5158 0116, www.visitmallacoota.com.au, 0900-1700.*

Buchan and around → *For listings, see pages 64-67.*

Tiny Buchan is best known for its limestone caves but it is also just south of the Snowy River National Park. Consequently it is a good area for walking, canoeing and rafting as well as caving. There are over 300 caves in the region, the best of which are contained in the **Buchan Caves Reserve** ① *entrance is just north of town, before the bridge, T131963, T5155 9264, Oct-Mar 1000, 1115, 1415 and 1530, Apr-Sep 1100, 1300 and 1500, $14, children $8, concessions $11.50,* which has two well-lit show caves with spectacular golden cave decorations. **Fairy Cave** and **Royal Cave** are famous for their pillars, stalactites, stalagmites, flowstone and calcite pools. There are 'adventure' caving tours, available during Easter and Christmas holidays or when numbers permit, and some good short walks. The 3-km **Spring Creek Walk** is a loop that heads uphill to Spring Creek Falls and passes through remnant rainforest, mossy rocks and ferns. Lyrebirds, kookaburras and parrots may be seen (or heard) on this track. Detailed walking notes and bookings for cave tours are available from the Parks Victoria office in the reserve. Limited information is available at the post office or general store in Buchan.

❂ Southeast Victoria listings

For Where to stay and Restaurant price codes and other relevant information, see pages 13-17.

🛏 Where to stay

Wilson's Promontory National Park *p60*
The Prom is so popular that accommodation is allocated by ballot for Dec-Jan (including campsites). Even at other times, weekends may have to be booked a year in advance. Also, check out www.promaccom.com.au.

$$$ Tingara View Tea House and Cottages, 10 Tingara Close, Yanakie, T5687 1488, www.promcountry.com.au/tingaraview. 3 pretty, colonial-style 1-room cottages with lovely views, cooked breakfast served in main house, also dinner and afternoon tea.

$$$-$$ Park cabin/campsite, T5680 9555, wprom@parks.vic.gov.au. The best place to stay is undoubtedly within the park itself. There is a good range of accommodation in cabins, units and huts.

Camping in the park is fantastic. There is an (unbookable) international campers area available for 1-2 nights.

Gippsland Lakes *p61*
In Bairnsdale there are a couple of caravan parks, and several motels and B&Bs. Accommodation may be plentiful in Lakes Entrance, but if you're travelling over Christmas and January, book well ahead.

$$$$-$$$ Déjà Vu, just to the north of Lakes Entrance over the lake on Clara St, T5155 4330, www.dejavu.com.au. This modern, glass-filled, hosted B&B, set in 7 acres of wild lakeside country, has rooms with private lake-view balconies, and the first-class service is friendly and attentive, with some unexpected and unusual flourishes. Also a couple of suitably alluring self-contained properties fronting the lake. Book well in advance. Lovely.

$$$ Anchorage, The Anchorage, Metung, T5156 2569, www.anchoragebedandbreakfast.com.au. Comfortable B&B with particularly wonderful wooden breakfast atrium.

$$$ BelleVue, 201 Esplanade, Lakes Entrance, T5155 3055, www.bellevuelakes.com. A cracking little daytime café and decent mid-range seafood restaurant help make this very comfortably furnished, family-run motel stand out from the crowd.

$$ Arendell cabins, Metung, T5156 2507, www.arendellmetung.com.au. There are various spacious, self-contained options, set in lawned gardens.

$$ Bellbrae, 4 km out on Ostlers Rd, Lakes Entrance, T5155 2319, www.lakes-entrance.com/bellbrae. Similar cabins to **Arendell**, but cheaper and better spaced out in a forest setting.

$$ Lazy Acre, 35 Roadknight St, Lakes Entrance, T5155 1323, www.lazyacre.com. Several well-maintained and self-contained log cabins, one specifically designed for the disabled, each sleeping up to 6.

$$ Old Pub, Esplanade, Paynesville, T5156 6442. Five pub rooms, unusually all en suite, freshly decorated and furnished, continental breakfast, pleasant veranda. Bistro with a cheap menu, superb salad and veggie bar.

$ Riviera Backpackers, 669 Esplanade, Lakes Entrance, T5155 2444, www.yha com.au. Very well-run and well-equipped YHA hostel with a good range of rooms, including several doubles (some en suite), all at a good-value-per-head price. Cheap bike hire, pool. Friendly and knowledgeable owners.

East to Mallacoota *p62*
If using Orbost as a base for exploring the local national parks, the most interesting place to stay is out on the Buchan Rd. Most of the accommodation in Mallacoota is

self-contained holiday flats or caravan parks. Book ahead for Dec-Jan and during Carnival.

$$$$ Point Hicks Lighthouse Keepers' Cottages, T5156 0432, www.pointhicks. com.au. In Croajingolong National Park, with verandas overlooking the sea, sleeps 8. Pricey, very comfortable and heavily booked at peak times. If free the managers may offer a 'rock-up rate' of $100 double or offer accommodation to backpackers in a simple bungalow. Call in advance to arrange an unlocked gate.

$$$$-$$ Karbeethong Lodge, 16 Schnapper Point Dr, Mallacoota, T5158 0411, www.karbeethonglodge.com.au. Comfortable old guesthouse, 4 km north of the town centre, with wide verandas overlooking the inlet, 12 rooms, some with en suite, communal kitchen facility. Not suitable for kids.

$$$-$$ Adobe Mudbrick Flats, 14 Karbeethong Hill Av, just north of the Lodge, Mallacoota, T5158 0329, www.adobeholidayflats.com.au. 10 original and delightful hand-built self-contained flats with superb views of the inlet. Countless birds, possums and even koalas share this 28-ha property. The very welcoming, knowledgeable hosts help make a stay here a real experience.

$$$-$$ Marlo Hotel, 19 Argyle Pde, Marlo, T5154 8201. An impressive pub and guesthouse with en suites. An 11,000-ha, relatively undisturbed park extends from Cape Conran up to the Croajingolong.

$$-$ Mallacoota, 51 Maurice Av, Mallacoota, T5158 0455. Lively pub, particularly on a Fri, serves cheap light lunches and mid-range dinners, including a good range of vegetarian options. They have 20 motel rooms and also a few shared rooms designated for backpackers with a small but clean kitchen. Food daily 1200-1345 and 1800-2000.

$$-$ Parks Victoria, T131963/T5154 8438, www.parksvic.gov.au. Manages cabins at

Cape Conran, sleeping up to 6 people, and a camping ground with fireplaces, toilets and bush showers. At peak times cabins are allocated by lottery, and campsites are booked months in advance.

Camping Campsites in Croajingolong National Park must be booked at the parks office. Book well in advance for Dec-Jan and Easter. The main camping areas are all situated where rivers and creeks meet the coast, **Thurra River** (46 sites) and **Wingan Inlet** (24 sites) both have stunning locations but the sites are close together and do get very busy in peak summer and holiday periods. It's still sleepy in comparison to the Prom though!

Mallacoota has excellent camping parks including the **$$-$ Foreshore**, T5158 0300, www.mallacootaholidaypark.com.au, the **$$-$ Shady Gully**, Lot 5, Mallacoota-Genoa Rd, T5158 0362 and the **$$-$ Wangralea**, 78 Betka Rd, T5158 0222. The latter has a camp kitchen.

Buchan and around *p63*

$$$ Snowy River Wildernest, T5154 1923, www.snowyriverwildernest.com. An isolated 150-ha deer farm, 30 km towards Orbost, snuggled in a wooded valley on a beautiful stretch of the Snowy River, with 2 spacious but basic self-contained houses, sleeping 11 and 10. The cheap restaurant is in a rustic terrace by the main homestead that is friendly and cosy.

$$ Buchan Valley Log Cabins, Gelantipy Rd, just over the bridge, Buchan, T5155 9494, www.buchanlogcabins.com.au. Self-contained, 2-bedroom cabins, set on a hillside overlooking the valley. Serviceable furnishings, large deck.

$ Buchan Lodge, Saleyard Rd, heading north, take first left after the bridge, Buchan, T5155 9421, www.buchanlodge.com. Excellent pine-log backpackers' hostel with warm, homely open kitchen and dining hall. Peaceful, rural location.

Camping $$-$ There is a camping ground in the Buchan Caves Reserve with cabins, bookings at the Parks Office, T5155 9264.

🍴 Restaurants

Wilson's Promontory National Park *p60*
Places to eat in the park are limited to lack-lustre fast food from the café at Tidal River or **Yanakie's Roadhouse**; the closest decent food is in Fish Creek or Foster. There is also a shop at Tidal River stocking a limited range of groceries and petrol.

$$ Fishy Pub, on the highway, Fish Creek, T5683 2404. Daily 1200-1400, 1800-2000. Excellent food, also live music most weekends.

$$ Koonwarra Store, Koonwarra, T5664 2285. Daily 0800-1700, wine bar and diner Fri-Sat 1830-2130. Café/restaurant serving country breakfasts, lunches and dinners of the highest quality, and a takeaway. Book for meals at weekends.

$ Rhythm, 3 Bridge St, Foster, T5682 1612. Thu-Tue 0900-1700, daily 1800-2100 in peak summer. There aren't many places to eat but this café is excellent. Scrumptious breakfasts, casual lunches and cakes in a small, bright jazzy room.

Gippsland Lakes *p61*
$$ Espas, Raymond Island, near Paynesville, T/F5156 7275. Fri-Sat 1000-2030, Sun 1000-1700. Excellent modern food in this striking place with an outdoor deck facing Paynesville across the water.

$$ Miriam's, 3 Bulmer St, Lakes Entrance, T5155 3999. 1800-2130. First-floor, funky restaurant, great balcony tables in summer, abundant candles and candelabras in the darker months. Good seafood.

$$-$ Fisherman's Wharf Pavilion,
Paynesville, T5156 0366. Right on the water and a wonderful spot either summer or winter. A café by day with breakfasts and interesting light lunches, mid-range restaurant Thu-Sat to 2000.

$$-$ L'Ocean Fish and Chips, 19 Myer St, Lakes Entrance, T5155 2253. The best fish and chips in town.

$$-$ Marrillee, 50 Metung Rd, Metung, T5156 2121. Open breakfast, lunch and dinner. One of very few choices in the village, but good seafood none the less. Open fireplaces inside and out. Licensed.

$$-$ Wyanga Park Winery, 10 km north of Lakes Entrance on Baades Rd, T5155 1508, www.wyangapark.com.au. Tastings and a colourful, characterful café open daily 1000-1700, doubling as a restaurant, Thu-Sat 1800-2000.

$ Central, Lakes Entrance. Daily 1200-1400, 1800-2000. A pub with a large bistro area. Surprisingly good meals, with a self-service salad and veggie bar.

$ Other than that you will find plenty of traditional cafés and fish and chip shops along the Esplanade.

⛰ What to do

Wilson's Promontory National Park *p60*
Bunyip Tours, T9650 9680,
www.bunyiptours.com. An eco-friendly outfit that takes small groups out to Wilson's Promontory and Phillip Island. It offers 1- to 2-day guided or unguided treks, with hostel stays (camping only at Wilson's Prom) included (2 days Phillip Island and Wilson's Prom, $280). Equipment – bar sleeping bags and a backpack – and food included.
Wildlife Coast Cruises, T5952 5583, www.wildlifecoastcruises.com.au. Runs occasional day cruises from Port Welshpool that include stops at Waterloo Bay, Refuge Cove and cruising around the lighthouse, Skull Rock and a seal colony (Port Welshpool, $180, 7 hrs, half-day option $78).

Gippsland Lakes *p61*
Virtually all activity revolves around the water, with several ways of getting out onto the 100s of square kilometres of lakes.

Clint's Ski School, Paynesville, T0427-825416. Offers good-value private lessons, multiple runs for the more experienced and ski-tube runs. Equipment supplied.

Lakes Entrance Paddle Boats, over the footbridge in Lakeside to the spit, T0419-552753. Provides anything from a body board to a small catamaran, hourly/daily hire.

Riviera Nautic, Metung, T5156 2243, www.rivieranautic.com.au. Highly regarded operator offering various overnight motor-cruisers and sailboats for hire, from around $500 a day (minimum 2 days), which is the best way to experience the lakes.

Victor Hire Boats, Marine Parade, T5155 3988. Motorboats can be hired from here.

East to Mallacoota *p62*

Mallacoota Explorer Tours, T0408 315615/ T5158 0116, ww.mallacootaexplorer. com.au. Offers popular 2-hr scenic and historic tours that connect with V-Line Coach services, T136196, in Genoa twice daily Tue, Thu and Sun.

To explore the inlet at Mallacoota: *MV Lochard*, Mallacoota, T5158 0764, is an old ferryboat taking larger groups on 2- to 3-hr cruises around the inlet from $28, while *The Porkie Bess*, Mallacoota, T5158 0109, is a smaller wooden affair built in 1947, skippered by a knowledgeable local.

The VIC can supply the latest charter listings, T5151 0116.

Buchan and around *p63*

Adventurama, T9819 1311, www.adventurama.com.au. Abseiling, caving and rafting. Their full day rafting options range from $155-$245, while the full 7-day Snowy River experience will cost you around $1950; full day abseiling and caving from $175.

Transport

Wilson's Promontory *p60*

The 200-km drive from Melbourne via the South Gippsland Highway, turning south at Meeniyan and Fish Creek, or Foster, takes about 3 hrs. Tidal River, where the main visitor facilities are, is 30 km inside the park boundary. There are limited services to the Prom from Melbourne and Foster; for detailed train information contact **V-Line**, T136196, www.vline.com.au and for bus services between Foster and Tidal River contact Moon's Buslines, T5687 1249.

Gippsland Region *p61*

For bus service timetables and fares throughout the Gippsland region contact **V-Line**, T136196, www.vlinepassenger. com.au, or the local VIC.

Contents

Footnotes

A sprint through history

1606 Spaniard Luis de Torres negotiates his way through the strait between Australia and New Guinea, becoming the first European to glimpse the Australian mainland.

1642 Dutchman Abel Tasman charts the northwest coast of what is now called New Holland. He also finds Tasmania before heading west to 'discover' New Zealand.

1770 Captain James Cook charts the hitherto unexplored east coast of New Holland. He names the 'new territory' New South Wales.

1786 Following the loss of the American colonies, the British government decides to transport felons instead to New South Wales. The following year Arthur Phillip's 'First Fleet' sets out.

1787-1788 Botany Bay is not to Phillip's liking so he explores the harbour just to the north, Port Jackson. Sydney Cove is duly named as the site for the new penal colony.

1801-1803 Matthew Flinders charts the unknown southern coasts and circumnavigates the whole continent in 1801-1803, proving it at last to be one vast island. He also suggests the name Australia for this new continent.

1830s Numbers of new settlers steadily increase as New South Wales slowly comes to be seen as a land of opportunity. Wool becomes the single most important industry and the Australian sheep population rockets. This is the catalyst for the Murray steamboats, the railways and new non-penal towns.

1850 The Aboriginal population is decimated by various infectious diseases against which the native Australians have little defence. Meanwhile, wool and grain industries are booming and coal and copper are being profitably mined.

1850-1860 Gold is first publicly found in New South Wales and soon after in Victoria, leading to a mass influx of would-be prospectors.

1860 Transportation of convicts ends. Nearly 160,000 had made the enforced trip over the previous 60-odd years, with few returning to their homelands.

1860-1890 Australia's own industrial revolution is in full flow and urbanization of the country continues apace. The indigenous population meanwhile is driven to the margins of society.

1889 NSW prime minister suggests political federation. Two years later a draft constitution is drawn up.

1893 Falling prices lead to an economic crash of unprecedented proportions. Victoria suffers the worst and the state government revives the idea of federation.

1897 Queensland Aborigines Act is introduced. Aboriginal people in the state can be forced to move to a reserve, denied alcohol and the vote, and are paid for work under conditions and wages stipulated by the act.

1898-1900 Colonies vote for federation.

1901 The Commonwealth officially comes into existence on 1 January. Melbourne is the first capital, remaining so until 1927 when Canberra is built.

1902 Women are given the vote.

1914-1918 First World War. Australian (and NZ) troops feature in many campaigns, most famously at Gallipoli, in 1915. Of the 300,000 who go to war, more than 50,000 are killed, a greater number than is lost by the USA.

1927 Canberra's Parliament House opens.

1932 Sydney Harbour Bridge is completed.

1933-1939 Aboriginal Act passed in QLD permits marriage and sexual relations between Aboriginal people and Europeans, with the aim of ultimately 'breeding out' the Aboriginal race.

1939-1945 Second World War. Australia sends troops to Europe. In 1942 Japanese bombers and warships shell Darwin, Sydney and Newcastle. In the same year, Australian troops help prevent occupation of Port Moresby in New Guinea. Out of a population of around seven million in 1939, a little under one million are enlisted or conscripted, of which nearly 40,000 are killed. Over 2000 Aborigines fight in the defence of their country.

1945- The government pursues a vigorous population programme. Tens of thousands of European economic migrants pour into the country. Many form ghettos in suburbs of Sydney and Melbourne.

1949 Robert Menzies leads his new Liberal party to election victory. A staunch monarchist, he welcomes Queen Elizabeth II to Australia in 1954, the first reigning monarch to make the trip. Immigration policies continue apace. Between 1945 and 1973 about three and a half million people arrive.

1956 Melbourne hosts the Olympic Games.

1960s Australia sends 8000 troops to fight with the USA in Vietnam, marking a growing shift from British influence. Protest movement against the war is broadened to include Aboriginal people. In the early 1960s new legislation largely removes the paternalistic and restrictive laws relating to Aboriginal people. In 1967 Australians vote in a referendum to allow the federal government to legislate for Aboriginal people.

1972 The Labor Party is elected under charismatic and energetic Gough Whitlam. Within days the troops are recalled from Vietnam and conscription ended, women are legally granted an equal wage structure, 'White Australia' is formally abandoned, a Ministry of Aboriginal Affairs created and 'God Save the Queen' scrapped as the national anthem.

1970s and 1980s Whitlam is sacked in controversial circumstances but he has permanently altered the mood of the nation. The fledgling Green movement begins to make its mark, and 1978 sees Sydney's first Gay and Lesbian march, which will become the Mardi Gras, the biggest event of its kind in the world. The country opens its doors to thousands of Vietnamese boat people.

1988 Australia celebrates the Bicentennial – 200 years of white settlement. Aboriginal people do not join the celebrations.

1992 The High Court rules that native title (or prior indigenous ownership of land) is not extinguished by the Crown's claim of possession in the Murray Islands of Torres Strait. This is enshrined in the Native Title Act of 1993.

1996-1998 The High Court rules that pastoral leases and native title can co-exist but the government of John Howard is opposed. A compromise, the Native Title Amendment Bill, is passed in 1998. In 1997, the Human Rights and Equal Opportunity Commission produces a damning report into the separation of Aboriginal and Torres Strait Islander children from their families and recommends compensation, counselling and an official apology.

1999 'No' vote in a national referendum for an Australian republic, despite polls showing a majority in favour.

2000 The Council for Aboriginal Reconciliation presents a Declaration of Reconciliation to the government. In the same year there are large reconciliation marches all over the country. The Olympics are held in Sydney. The Aboriginal athlete Kathy Freeman wins gold in the women's 400 m track sprint.

2001-2002 Bushfires ravage the surrounding national parks and fringes of Sydney, destroying numerous properties and taking several lives. In 2002, exacerbated by severe drought conditions, Victoria suffers its worst fires for years.

2001 The Liberal-National coalition government of John Howard is returned to power. In the same year, a Norwegian vessel rescues boat people claiming to be refugees from Afghanistan but the Australian government refuses to allow the 'illegal immigrants' to land on the mainland. This not only diminishes Australia's international standing but also polarizes society.

2002 Two nightclubs are bombed in Bali, killing around 200 people, almost half of whom are Australian. Prime Minister Howard continues to support the US invasion of Iraq, despite majority public opposition domestically.

2005 A second terrorist bomb in Bali kills 19.

2006-2007 Australia suffers its worst drought on record. As a result the government slashes economic growth forecasts, reflecting a slump in farm output. Prime Minister John Howard still dismisses the Kyoto Climate Change Protocol and joins the USA in its refusal to sign.

2007 After 11 years at the helm Prime Minister John Howard and his coalition party suffer an unexpected defeat. Kevin Rudd's Labor Party takes the reins, promising a dramatic change of direction in federal climate change policy and a definitive phased withdrawal of the Australian armed forces in Iraq.

2009-2012 On the back of a resources boom fuelled by China and India's rapacious economic development and thanks to sound banking practices Australia survives the worst of the global financial crisis. In 2010 it emerges with the strongest economic growth forecasts of all developed nations. As a result the Australian dollar also becomes one of the strongest world currencies, almost reaching parity with the US dollar and rising by almost 20% against the UK pound. The strength of the Australian dollar impacts tourism, with fewer international arrivals and a rapid rise in Australians holidaying overseas.

In June 2010 Deputy Prime Minister Julia Gillard takes over from Rudd and becomes leader of the Labour Party and the first female Prime Minister of Australia. She again defeats Rudd in a leadership ballot in 2012. The next elections will take place in 2013.

Wildlife in East Coast Australia

Wildlife is very much a part of the Australian holiday experience. Living icons like the koala and kangaroo are just as ingrained in our psyche as the famous Opera House or Uluru (Ayers Rock). The list of species reads like a who's who of the marvellous, bizarre and highly unlikely. There are over 750 bird species alone. The following is a very brief description of the species you are most likely to encounter on your travels.

Marsupials

Marsupials (derived from the Latin word *marsupium* meaning 'pouch') can be described as mammals that have substituted the uterus with the teat. Their reproductive system is complex, the females have not one but three vaginas and there is a short gestation and a long lactation. It is a specialist system, developed to meet harsh environmental demands.

The most famous of the marsupials are of course the kangaroos and wallabies. There are over 50 species of kangaroos, wallabies and tree kangaroos in Australia. The most commonly seen are the eastern grey and the red. The eastern grey can be seen almost anywhere in New South Wales, Queensland and Victoria, especially in the wildlife and national parks along the coast. Sadly in the outback most of the red kangaroos you see will be roadkill. Tree kangaroos, meanwhile, live deep in the bush and are notoriously shy and are therefore very seldom seen.

Equally famous is the koala (which is not a bear). Koalas are well adapted to the harsh Australian environment, surviving quite happily on one of the most toxic of leaves – eucalyptus. Koalas are easily encountered in the many wildlife parks throughout the country but, while cuddling one of these impossibly cute bundles of fur is the most seminal Australian experience, do bear in mind that the wild variety may take exception to being manhandled and attempt to rip your arms to shreds. Sadly, koalas are on the decline in most regions of Australia and over 80% of their natural habitat has been destroyed since white settlement began.

There are three species of wombat: the common, northern and southern hairy-nosed variety. Like the koala, they are very well adapted to the Australian environment and spend much of their time asleep. They are also nocturnal. Campsites are the best places to see them, where burrows and small piles of dung will provide testimony to their presence. Sadly, like kangaroos and koalas, they are far more commonly seen as roadkill. Another familiar family member of the marsupials is the possum. There are numerous species, with the most commonly encountered being the doe-eyed brushtail possum and the smaller ring-tailed possum. Both are common in urban areas and regularly show up after dusk in campsites. Another magnificent little possum that may be seen is the squirrel-sized feather-tailed glider, which as the name suggests can glide from tree to tree. All the possum species are nocturnal, hence the huge eyes. The best way to see them is by joining a night spotting tour, especially in Queensland, where in only a hectare or two of bush there may be as many as 18 different species. Other marsupials include the rare and meat-eating tiger quoll, which is about the size of a cat with a brownish coat dotted with attractive white spots, the delightful quokka (like a miniature wallaby), bandicoots, the numbat (endangered) and the bilby.

Monotremes

There are only three living species of monotremes in the world: the duck-billed platypus and the short-beaked echidna, both of which are endemic to Australia, and the long-beaked echidna, found only on the islands of New Guinea. Their name meaning 'one hole', refers to their birdlike cloaca, and their most remarkable feature is that they are mammals that lay eggs.

The duck-billed platypus is found only in rivers and freshwater lakes in eastern Australia. They live in burrows, are excellent swimmers and can stay submerged for up to 10 minutes. The duck-like bill is not hard like the beak of a bird, but soft and covered in sensitive nerve endings that help to locate food. The males have sharp spurs on both hind leg ankles that can deliver venom strong enough to cause excruciating pain in humans and even kill a dog. Platypuses are best seen just before dawn.

The echidna is not related to the hedgehog but looks decidedly like one. You will almost certainly encounter the echidna all over Australia, even in urban areas, where they belligerently go about their business and are a delight to watch. They are immensely powerful creatures not dissimilar to small spiny tanks. They are mainly nocturnal and hunt for insects by emitting electrical signals from their long snout, before catching them with a long sticky tongue.

Eutherians

Eutherians are placental mammals. Perhaps the best known is the dingo. Although not strictly endemic to Australia, having being introduced, most probably by Aboriginals over 3000-4000 years ago and derived from an Asian wild dog, they are now seen to be as Australian as Fosters lager. Found everywhere on the continent, but absent from Tasmania, they are highly adaptable, opportunist carnivores, which makes them highly unpopular with farmers. The best place to see dingoes is on Fraser Island, off Queensland, where sadly they have come into conflict with humans due to scavenging.

The mighty fruit bat is another placental mammal and a remarkable creature that you will almost certainly see (or smell) on your travels. You can even see them flying around at dusk on the fringes of Sydney's CBD (especially the Botanical Gardens).

Birds

With one of the most impressive bird lists in the world, Australia is a birdwatcher's paradise and even the most indifferent cannot fail to be impressed by their diversity, colours and calls. The most famous of Australian birds is the kookaburra, which is related to the kingfisher. Other than its prevalence, fearlessness and extrovert behaviour, it is its laughing call that marks it out. A much stranger-looking specimen is the tawny frogmouth, a kind of cross between an owl and a frog, with camouflaged plumage, fiery orange eyes and a mouth the size of the Channel Tunnel. Due to its nocturnal lifestyle it is hard to observe in the wild and is best seen in zoos and wildlife parks.

Australia is famous for its psittacines – the parrot family – including parakeets, lorikeets, cockatiels, rosellas and budgerigars, which can be seen at their most impressive in the outback, in huge flocks against the vast blue sky. The rainbow lorikeet is a common sight (and sound) in urban areas, while in rural areas and forests the graceful red- white- and yellow-tailed black cockatoos are also a pleasure to behold. Others include the pink galah, the breathtaking king parrot and the evocatively named gang-gang.

Almost as colourful are the bowerbirds. There are several species in Australia, the most notable being the beautiful but endangered regent bowerbird, with its startling gold and black plumage, and the satin bowerbird. Another member of the bowerbird family is the catbird, which, once heard, proves to be very aptly named.

In the bush one of the commonest of birds is the brush turkey, about the size of a chicken, with a bare head and powerful legs and feet. Another well-known bird of the bush is the lyrebird, of which there are two species in Australia. Unremarkable in appearance (rather like a bantam) though truly remarkable in their behaviour, they are expert mimics and often fool other birds into thinking there are others present protecting territory. Their name derives from the shape of their tail (males only) which when spread out looks like the ancient Greek musical instrument.

A far larger, rarer bird of the tropical rainforest is the cassowary, a large flightless relative of the emu with a mantle of black hair-like plumage, colourful wattles and a strange, blunt horn on its head. It is a highly specialist feeder of forest fruits and seeds. Tragically, roadkills are common. Their last remaining stronghold in Australia is in Far North Queensland, especially around Mission Beach, where they are keenly protected. They are well worth seeing but your best chance of doing so remains in wildlife sanctuaries and zoos.

Almost as large, yet flighted, and more often seen around lakes and wetlands, are the brolga and the black-necked stork, or jaribu. The brolga is a distinctly leggy, grey character with a dewlap (flap of skin under the chin) and a lovely splash of red confined to its head. The brolga is equally leggy but has a lovely iridescent purple-green neck set off with a daffodil-yellow eye and rapier-like beak. One of the most impressive birds is the white-breasted sea eagle, which is a glorious sight almost anywhere along the coast or around inland lakes and waterways. They are consummate predators and highly adept at catching fish with their incredibly powerful talons.

The fairy penguin, found all along the southern coastline of Australia, is the smallest penguin in the world. The largest colony is on Phillip Islands near Melbourne, where over 20,000 are known to breed in a vast warren of burrows. The emu, with its long powerful legs, is prevalent yet quite shy, unlike that other giant of the outback, the huge wedge-tailed eagle (or 'wedgie'). Wedgies are most commonly sighted feeding on roadkills, especially kangaroos.

Reptiles, amphibians and insects

The range of reptile, amphibian and insect species is, not surprisingly, as diverse as any other in Australia. First up is the crocodile. There are two species in Australia, the saltwater crocodile (or 'saltie' as they are known) found throughout the Indo-Australian region, and the smaller freshwater crocodile, which is endemic. There is no doubt the mighty saltie is, along with the great white shark, the most feared creature on earth and perhaps deservedly so. Although you will undoubtedly encounter crocodiles in zoos, wildlife parks and farms throughout the country, you may also be lucky (or unlucky) enough to spot one in the wild in the northern regions. Note that in Queensland the many warning signs next to rivers and estuaries are there for a good reason.

The goanna, or monitor, is a common sight, especially in campsites, where their belligerence is legendary. There are actually many species of goanna in Australia. They can reach up to 2 m in length, are carnivores and if threatened, run towards anything upright to escape. Of course, this is usually a tree, but not always, so be warned!

There are many species of frogs and toads in Australia including the commonly seen green tree frog. They are a beautiful lime-green colour. If you find one do not handle them since the grease on our hands can damage their sensitive skin. Another character worth mentioning is the banjo frog. If you are ever in the bush and are convinced you can hear someone plucking the strings of a banjo, it is probably a banjo frog singing to its mate.

Insects are well beyond the scope of this handbook, but there are two that, once encountered, will almost certainly never be forgotten. The first is the huntsman spider, a very common species seen almost anywhere in Australia, especially indoors. Although not the largest spider on the continent, they can grow to a size that would comfortably cover the palm of your hand. Blessed with the propensity to shock, they are an impressive sight, do bite, but only when provoked and are not venomous. Of the huge variety of glorious butterflies and moths in Australia perhaps the most beautiful is the Ulysses blue, found in the tropics, especially in Far North Queensland.

Marine mammals and turtles

Along both the eastern and western seaboards of Australia humpback whales are commonly sighted on their passage to and from the tropics to Antarctica between the months of July and October. Occasionally they are even seen wallowing in Sydney Harbour or breaching the waters off the famous Bondi Beach. The southern right whale is another species regularly seen in Australian waters; likewise the orca, or killer whale. Several species of dolphin are present, including the bottlenose dolphin, which is a common sight off almost any beach surfing the waves with as much skill and delight as any human on a surfboard.

Another less well-known sea mammal, clinging precariously to a few locales around the coast, is the dugong or sea cow. Cardwell and the waters surrounding Hinchinbrook Island, in Queensland, remains one of the best places to see them. Australia is also a very important breeding ground for turtles. The Mon Repos Turtle Rookery, Queensland, is one of the largest and most important loggerhead turtle rookeries in the world. A visit during the nesting season from October to May, when the females haul themselves up at night to lay their eggs, or the hatchlings emerge to make a mad dash for the waves, is a truly unforgettable experience.

Index

Titles available in the Footprint *Focus* range

Latin America	UK RRP	US RRP
Bahia & Salvador	£7.99	$11.95
Brazilian Amazon	£7.99	$11.95
Brazilian Pantanal	£6.99	$9.95
Buenos Aires & Pampas	£7.99	$11.95
Cartagena & Caribbean Coast	£7.99	$11.95
Costa Rica	£8.99	$12.95
Cuzco, La Paz & Lake Titicaca	£8.99	$12.95
El Salvador	£5.99	$8.95
Guadalajara & Pacific Coast	£6.99	$9.95
Guatemala	£8.99	$12.95
Guyana, Guyane & Suriname	£5.99	$8.95
Havana	£6.99	$9.95
Honduras	£7.99	$11.95
Nicaragua	£7.99	$11.95
Northeast Argentina & Uruguay	£8.99	$12.95
Paraguay	£5.99	$8.95
Quito & Galápagos Islands	£7.99	$11.95
Recife & Northeast Brazil	£7.99	$11.95
Rio de Janeiro	£8.99	$12.95
São Paulo	£5.99	$8.95
Uruguay	£6.99	$9.95
Venezuela	£8.99	$12.95
Yucatán Peninsula	£6.99	$9.95

Asia	UK RRP	US RRP
Angkor Wat	£5.99	$8.95
Bali & Lombok	£8.99	$12.95
Chennai & Tamil Nadu	£8.99	$12.95
Chiang Mai & Northern Thailand	£7.99	$11.95
Goa	£6.99	$9.95
Gulf of Thailand	£8.99	$12.95
Hanoi & Northern Vietnam	£8.99	$12.95
Ho Chi Minh City & Mekong Delta	£7.99	$11.95
Java	£7.99	$11.95
Kerala	£7.99	$11.95
Kolkata & West Bengal	£5.99	$8.95
Mumbai & Gujarat	£8.99	$12.95

Africa & Middle East	UK RRP	US RRP
Beirut	£6.99	$9.95
Cairo & Nile Delta	£8.99	$12.95
Damascus	£5.99	$8.95
Durban & KwaZulu Natal	£8.99	$12.95
Fès & Northern Morocco	£8.99	$12.95
Jerusalem	£8.99	$12.95
Johannesburg & Kruger National Park	£7.99	$11.95
Kenya's Beaches	£8.99	$12.95
Kilimanjaro & Northern Tanzania	£8.99	$12.95
Luxor to Aswan	£8.99	$12.95
Nairobi & Rift Valley	£7.99	$11.95
Red Sea & Sinai	£7.99	$11.95
Zanzibar & Pemba	£7.99	$11.95

Europe	UK RRP	US RRP
Bilbao & Basque Region	£6.99	$9.95
Brittany West Coast	£7.99	$11.95
Cádiz & Costa de la Luz	£6.99	$9.95
Granada & Sierra Nevada	£6.99	$9.95
Languedoc: Carcassonne to Montpellier	£7.99	$11.95
Málaga	£5.99	$8.95
Marseille & Western Provence	£7.99	$11.95
Orkney & Shetland Islands	£5.99	$8.95
Santander & Picos de Europa	£7.99	$11.95
Sardinia: Alghero & the North	£7.99	$11.95
Sardinia: Cagliari & the South	£7.99	$11.95
Seville	£5.99	$8.95
Sicily: Palermo & the Northwest	£7.99	$11.95
Sicily: Catania & the Southeast	£7.99	$11.95
Siena & Southern Tuscany	£7.99	$11.95
Sorrento, Capri & Amalfi Coast	£6.99	$9.95
Skye & Outer Hebrides	£6.99	$9.95
Verona & Lake Garda	£7.99	$11.95

North America	UK RRP	US RRP
Vancouver & Rockies	£8.99	$12.95

Australasia	UK RRP	US RRP
Brisbane & Queensland	£8.99	$12.95
Perth	£7.99	$11.95

For the latest books, e-books and a wealth of travel information, visit us at:
www.footprinttravelguides.com.

footprinttravelguides.com

Join us on facebook for the latest travel news, product releases, offers and amazing competitions:
www.facebook.com/footprintbooks